Play To Your Strengths

ANDY WHIPP

For my 3 girls

CONTENTS OVERVIEW

1   INTRO   Page 1

2   WHY ME?   Page 4

3   FAIL TO PLAN, PLAN TO FAIL   Page 18

4   PLAY TO YOUR STRENGTHS   Page 30

5   SUPER-STRENGTHS   Page 67

6   THE COMMITMENT COMMODITY   Page 81

7   EFFORT = REWARD   Page 90

8   BOUNCE BACK FROM A SETBACK   Page 117

9   ANYONE FOR CONSULTANCY?   Page 129

10 FINAL THOUGHTS   Page 135

ACKNOWLEDGEMENTS   Page 145

NOTES   Page 147

INDEX   Page 152

DETAILED CONTENTS

1:      INTRO   1

2:      WHY ME?   4

        Squash: Not just a vegetable   5

        When I was younger, so much younger than today   6

        Getting into the groove   7

        Hooray for Henry   10

        To be or not to be   12

        A real job – almost   15

        I wanna be startin' somethin'   16

3:      FAIL TO PLAN, PLAN TO FAIL   18

        Don't speculate – strategize   19

        Mr Motivator   20

        Step 1: The writing's on the wall   22

        Step 2: Going for goald   26

        Make the impossible possible   28

        The right goal for you   29

4:      PLAY TO YOUR STRENGTHS   30

        Self-help or the lack of…   31

        Everyone has a USP   32

Inferiority complex anyone?   33

Be the artist not the paint   36

Conquering confidence   37

Stack the deck in your favour   39

An Achiever believer   43

Let's get physical   48

What are your strengths?   48

Not an Achiever or solo artist?   50

Case studies   51

Confidence revisited   56

Partners in crime   57

Turn possibility into probability   59

What about weaknesses?   60

Pass the baton   62

So…   64

5:   **SUPER-STRENGTHS**   **67**

Jack of all trades but master of none   69

The wildcard   71

A wolf in squash clothing   73

Specialize not compromise   76

So…   78

6:	**THE COMMITMENT COMMODITY**	**81**
	New year, new excuses	82
	Monkey business	83
	What a feeling, when we're dancing on the ceiling	88
	So…	88
7:	**EFFORT = REWARD**	**90**
	Talent is a myth	92
	A super street?	96
	There's no such thing as speedy boarding	101
	Deliberate practice	102
	Age is nothing but a number	109
	You play the way you practice	111
	White men can't jump	113
	Bounce	114
	So…	115
8:	**BOUNCE BACK FROM A SETBACK**	**117**
	Acceptance is mindfulness	118
	Bounce-back-ability	120
	The power of positive	125
	So…	127
9:	**ANYONE FOR CONSULTANCY?**	**129**
	Not so common sense	129

Trust me, I'm a consultant   131

Hidden in plain sight   133

10: FINAL THOUGHTS   **135**

Take control – set your goal   136

Do what you do best   137

Going from strength to super-strength   139

Your best friend and your enemy   140

All in good time   141

Will you crack or bounce back   142

The overlooked sense   143

Acknowledgements   **145**

Notes   **147**

Index   **152**

1 INTRODUCTION

Success: The accomplishment of an aim or purpose.

Success must be personal. Success isn't measured by a universal achievement, it is unique to every individual.

"The reason your life stays the same is because you think everyone else is the problem. Your life can only change to the degree that you accept responsibility for it."

Dr STEVE MARABOLI

Myth - the reason we're not succeeding, not achieving, is because of someone else or something else beyond our control.

Truth - it is only our own limiting perceptions or beliefs which hold us back from making significant progress.

"It's always easy to blame others. You can spend your entire life blaming the world, but your successes or failures are entirely your own responsibility."

PAUL COELHO

I believe everybody is capable of performing better and without the need to go on any new and highly expensive courses in order to do so. There is no need to change who we are or to immediately learn any new skills. We all have strengths which remain underused. No matter what we do, what line of business we are in or want to be in, we have the potential to achieve fantastic results.

In this book we will examine the power of our strengths and the concept of creating super-strengths. Strengths can be a unique personal quality or a combination of traits we are born with, or it can be a specific quality in our particular field of expertise. Don't worry if you are yet to have a field of expertise; equally this book will help you to find your path to success. Together we will find the best path to take in order to succeed for each and every one of us.

With many documented cases outlining real life success-stories (including several close friends of mine), we will look into why they got to where they are today and how we can learn from their journeys. This book is not about becoming one of the richest people on the planet, but instead the focus is on HOW WE CAN IMPROVE OUR LIVES. Success isn't only seen in monetary rewards or by a full trophy cabinet, everyone should set their own goals, completely in keeping with their strengths and their desires whatever they may be. True success is in achieving our personal goals.

My purpose for this book is to inspire us all to take action in our lives. I want us to have the confidence and knowhow to perform better in our jobs. The message of this book has relevance for everyone; whatever type of profession or set of skills we have; whatever industry we may be in or are aspiring toward; whatever our age or past experience, my desire is to help maximize ourselves.

Everybody must create their own story by becoming the best version of themselves.

We are all unique with an exclusive set of skills. These skills are our USP (Unique Selling Point).

Embrace who you are.

"Winners and losers aren't born, they are the products of how they think"

LOU HOLTZ

So my question is this: Are you brave enough to instigate change in your life?

Now think about this: Unsuccessful people make decisions based on their current situation. Successful people make decisions based on where they want to be.

"I skate to where the puck is going to be, not to where it has been."

WAYNE GRETZKY

2 WHY ME?

Why me? Why do I think I can possibly help people? I do not have 40 years of business experience like Richard Branson or Warren Buffett. Nor have I got a 30 year history of self-help like Tony Robbins or Brian Tracy. I am not a billionaire. However, what I do have is experience from elite sport and how to integrate this in into business.

Sport and business are intrinsically linked. Businesses and entrepreneurs can learn a great deal from professional athletes, as can athletes can from businessmen and businesswomen. The personality of a professional athlete is particularly desirable in business. They are incredibly self-motivated. Every day they must display a level of determination and dedication that most humans could not contemplate doing, in order to give themselves the best possible chance of success. Imagine if we could bottle this formula of self-drive and discipline, then inject it into every single office worker in every office around the world? The results would be astounding, but alas, we can't! What we can do however is to make the most of what traits and skills we have to offer as individuals. What makes us unique can be extremely powerful. Without-a-doubt these unique skills can make us become an exceptional performer in whatever it is we want to do. Everyone can do it, there are no exceptions, and I want to show you how you can start your improvement today.

SQUASH: NOT JUST A VEGETABLE

"Squash is boxing with rackets."

JONAH BARRINGTON

I am an ex-professional squash player, a top squash coach and a businessman. I am the current British Masters Champion. I have coached a World No.1 squash player, a World Champion, several world top 10 players, as well as many other top professionals. I have my own sports clothing company, called AWsome Sports. I am a blogger with an ever growing fan base, and now I am a published author.

For those of you who don't know here's a little bit about squash: Squash is a fairly popular sport in the UK. It is among the top 10 most popular participation sports with over 500,000 people playing the sport on a regular basis on our small island. There are thousands of squash teams competing in various weekly leagues nationwide. Surprisingly 21% of working professionals choose squash as their preferred lunchtime workout beating tennis and going to the gym!

Squash is a sport which is rapidly growing worldwide, especially in countries like Egypt and North America. Around the globe more than 20 million people across 185 countries play squash regularly. Forbes magazine classifies squash as "the world's healthiest sport". This is based on cardiorespiratory endurance, muscular strength, flexibility, muscular endurance, calories burned, and risk of injury.

Squash is also considered to be one of the 3 toughest sports in the world to play professionally. It's often referred to as "physical chess" or "chess on legs", as each player tries to cleverly manoeuvre their opponent out of position with a combination of quick thinking and acquired skill, before delivering the killer blow… and all at over 100 mph. Understandably it is a particularly difficult sport to excel at and to become one of the world's elite.

Sadly squash is not a mainstream TV spectator sport, meaning the money involved for the top professionals compared to other sports (like soccer, golf and tennis to name a few) does not offer a fair reflection on the sport whatsoever. Saying that though, impressive sums can be earned by a certain few - the 'crème de la crème' - but we're talking the world's top 3 or 4 players only.

A few fun squash facts include: Elvis Presley was a regular squash and racketball player (usually playing in the early morning hours when he couldn't sleep!); there was a squash court and full time coach available on the ill-fated Titanic; Prince Philip played squash while Queen Elizabeth II was in labour (for 30 hours) giving birth to Prince Charles; and a not so fun fact - outrageously squash is not yet an Olympic sport, to the outrage of everyone involved. I won't get started on this subject because it will only get me mad!

Please do not worry however, this is most definitely not a book about squash, nor is it an autobiography about me. I am merely setting the scene as to my particular background. I believe elite squash, due to its physical requirements, provides the perfect environment for someone to develop an almost unparalleled task dedication and work ethic from a young age, and this is where my personal journey began....

WHEN I WAS YOUNGER, SO MUCH YOUNGER THAN TODAY

"The first thing is to love your sport. Never do it to please someone else. It has to be yours."

PEGGY FLEMING

I was always very sporty as a child. It didn't matter whether I was running around in a school PE lesson, kicking a soccer ball against our garage door (very much to the annoyance of our next door neighbour) or hitting a sponge ball in our hallway at Whitehaven Road - I just loved it. I began to play soccer for teams and clubs when I was 7 years old. I became decent at soccer to the joy of my mother who was an avid Manchester United fan. I began to play for my Beavers and Cubs teams (Beavers are like Scouts but for 6 to 8 year olds, and Cubs for ages 8 to 12), as well as all my school teams, and local junior clubs Mountfield Rovers and Bramhall North FC. I was a goalkeeper and generally stood out as one of the better performers. In my early teens I would get scouted by officials from top local senior clubs; Manchester United, Manchester City, Oldham Athletic and Crewe Alexandra.

At the age of 10 my Dad introduced me to squash as he thought I was getting too fat! Me and squash had an instant connection and before long I was competing in Under 12 (U12) competitions and representing my local county of Cheshire. When I was 12 I became aware of the England Squash National Ranking Lists, because somebody told me I was on it at the very bottom, at No.20 (England Squash only published the top 20 in my junior days; these days they show the top 200!). That was a big drive for me, knowing there was a whole community of kids my age competing in tournaments up and down the country, all for the prize of being the best in England - well actually, I suppose I should say everyone was doing it because they enjoyed it, not just to be the best, but not me however!

Right from the start I really did adore playing squash. It's a wonderful game, and unlike soccer, it's an individual sport - you take all the responsibility for your performance; on a bad day you take all the blame, but on a good day all the glory. My love of the game, coupled with my love of competing and the drive to become England Junior No.1, basically made me a squash addict from the moment I first picked up a racket.

GETTING INTO THE GROOVE

"Success is the sum of small efforts, repeated day-in, day-out."

ROBERT COLLIER

After finding out about the national ranking list at the age of 12, it gave me just under 2 years to get near the top of the Under 14's. I think I assumed I couldn't get to the top in 2 years as there were kids who had been playing since they were 4 years old, so in comparison I was a complete rookie. Saying that though, I had worked my way into the top 20 after just 2 years of playing, so maybe there was hope for me.

Before contemplating playing in national tournaments, firstly I had to find out the standard of junior squash players in my own county. My first rival was a boy from Cheshire called Brian Foster. He was a class act on the squash court and came from a real squash family. His Dad played, and his two older brothers played, and all three sons competed in competitions most weekends. Even at the age of 11 Brian had nearly a decade of experience, I was way off. I remember crying a few times after losing to Brian, but when I was 12 ½ I beat him. Then I set my sights to challenging his older brothers. Their dad must have hated me, and I genuinely think he did! I was close friends with all 3 boys for many years as we were valuable training partners to each other, especially with the oldest, Patrick. We trained a lot together when I was in my late teens. He became a professional squash player, reaching a decent world ranking high of 75.

I soon moved on to national events and after 2 years of playing tournaments all over the country, I was ranked No.2 in England for the U14 age group. Annoyingly I couldn't get that No.1 spot. I never had the chance to play the No.1, Jonathan Kemp. Kempy and I would have somewhat of an unspoken rivalry that would stay for quite a number of years. What's more, we were born just 1 week apart; my birthday's the 11th March 1981, and his is the 18th. This meant we would both go out of each junior age group on exactly the same month. (Coincidentally when we were 20, our Fathers both suddenly and unexpectedly died, and just two weeks apart. His Dad died on Thursday 31st January 2002 climbing Mount Kilimanjaro, and my Dad died of undiagnosed Heart Cancer 14 days later on Valentine's Day).

During these junior days, when I was between 12 and 16, I knew one day soon

I had to make a decision about my sport. Along with my increasingly busy squash schedule of daily training, weekly coaching, weekly league matches, weekend tournaments and Regional/National Training Squads, I was still enjoying playing soccer twice a week, and I also played cricket at the weekends. I'd even been asked to represent Cheshire as a wicket keeper and a number 3 batsman. Luckily cricket was a summer sport so it didn't clash with my squash tournaments (the squash season is the same as the soccer season in the UK; September to May). Squash and Soccer on the other hand would overlap from time to time. I vividly recall playing in squash tournaments, and not wanting to let down my soccer team whenever possible, me and my father would constantly dash from one venue to the next. We played our Bramhall North soccer matches on a Sunday morning, so if I was in a local squash event I would play my semi-final squash match early on the Sunday morning, rush off to my 90 minute soccer match, then rush back for the final, stepping on to court with dirty knees!

I had more-or-less known that squash was the sport for me, but this decision was finalized due to a couple of factors. With cricket, as I improved the bowling got extremely fast all of a sudden, so basically I was too much of a wimp for that! As for soccer, I was lacking in one major factor to be a top goalkeeper - height. Generally goalkeepers are at the very least 6 feet tall. I was not tall enough (at 5 foot 9) to play at a high level so Manchester United ended their interest in me. By a process of elimination I had my sport for life – Squash (which was the sport I loved the most anyway, and was best at).

Anyway back to my junior squash. I couldn't wait to get started in the U16 age group. I wanted that No.1 spot. After another 2 years of training, playing tournaments and relentless dedication on mine and my father's behalf, the March 1997 U16 England Rankings read, 1. Jonathan Kemp, 2. Andrew Whipp …. Doh!

Jon Kemp and I shared the same motivation, we both wanted to be the best. He was definitely seen as the England Squash 'Golden Child' with all sorts of funding, coaching and opportunities offered to him. I was left to my own devices, quietly doing my own thing. Although more expensive for my family, we preferred it this way. I had the coaching I wanted and played a style of squash I was most comfortable with. I was not confined by the

England Squash technique or game plan. I played to my strengths, not somebody else's. I always had the belief it would pay off.

The next age group was the U19, and after 3 years of competition and still loving every single event I played, the 1st March 2000 ranking list read, 1. Andrew Whipp, 2. Jonathan Kemp.

At last. I had done it!

HOORAY FOR HENRY

"My father gave me the greatest gift anyone could give another person, he believed in me."

JIM VALVANO

In all of this gallivanting around from squash court to squash court, my father was absolutely wonderful. Soccer was mainly mine and my Mum's thing, but squash was 100% me and Dad. He helped me to succeed because he genuinely believed I had the potential to be great. He also loved the fact that I had his natural drive and determination too.

Financially we were a very middle of the road family. I was lucky because he paid for everything I needed; the weekly lessons, the court fees, rackets, memberships, entry fees, hotels etc etc etc. However, the biggest thing he gave up for me was his time. He would drive me to the squash club every day and to tournaments most weekends so I could compete against the country's best. Every Thursday evening from the age of 12, I played regional Men's League matches (some over an hour drive away) which of course he also drove me to, and all this after he'd been fully exerting himself all day at work. Imagine how relieved he must have been when I turned 17 and could learn to drive for myself? Then, when I passed my driving test, out of love and support he bought me my own car, or maybe just to give himself a well-earned rest! It was a blue Ford Fiesta and it was absolutely perfect. For me a car was essential. Every week I would clock up hundreds of miles in pursuit of my squash dream.

Dad is without doubt, the cleverest man I have ever met. He did his O-Levels a year early and studied 2 years ahead at Cambridge University in his field of Maths and Mechanics. He told me a story once that his University professor (knowing he could not deliver the lecture that day) asked Henry to teach the lesson for him. This can't have been good for Dad's social life. I imagine his class mates must have hated him, especially as he was two years younger than them! It won't be a surprise for you to know that he finished University with a 'First', the top classification awarded from one of the most prestigious universities in the world.

Dad had a good job, it was reasonably well paid, but probably not one that merited a man of his intellect. It stressed him out big time. I really hope my squash was a good escape for him, but nevertheless for him to take me to squash, more or less every evening and weekend after his rubbish days at work, I will be eternally grateful.

My Dad, was himself an amazing sportsman in his day. At his boarding school and his University he was an incredibly fast runner, especially in the 100m, 200m and 400m distances. He ran the 100m in 11 seconds, the 200m in 21 seconds and 400m in 46 seconds. He also played a lot of rugby. I have always assumed he was like Forrest Gump, and once passed the rugby ball all his team mates would shout "run Henry, run". Bizarrely, athletics and rugby are two of my least favourite sports to compete in. Importantly though, he passed his sporty genes on to me. I inherited his powerful legs and big buttocks!

I used to love our road trips, driving up and down the UK to squash tournaments. It was here that Dad and I would talk about all kinds of nonsense. We loved to ponder and analyze. Any situation possible, we would question it. We would look to apply maths, science and logic to everything. We'd work out totally pointless things like how many blades of grass there were in a field or how much space a million pound coins would take up. He would get me thinking about many different things, for example; the news, cars, scientific discoveries, sport and space. My personal favourites were the concept of time and excellence in sport. It is definitely these types of conversations that have helped me to look at the world the way I do, and to look at people the way I do. It was these chats we'd have that have enabled my mind to plug into anything, no matter what the topic. Even if I was initially interested or not, I would always look to apply what I knew to figure it out. I guess it was these road trips which led me to write this book, so what you see in front of you I could say has been 25 years in the making!

TO BE OR NOT TO BE

"Have courage to follow your heart and intuition."

STEVE JOBS

At the age of 16 when I had made my decision to concentrate on squash, and to leave soccer and cricket behind, I knew I was going to be a professional player and squash would become my job. Squash had come to be a major part of my identity. It's the sport I loved. I wanted to be the best, and I knew I had a decent chance of doing so.

When it came to collage and A-Levels my interest in school began to wane. I already knew where my real passion was and it wasn't in the classroom. I'm sure my teachers rue the day I was placed in their classes with my lack of interest in what they had to say. In the end, after some last minute cramming my grades were fine, good enough at least to go to University. For me, University was an opportunity to go out on my own, party a bit and play even more squash. I combined University with playing the world Professional Squash Tour (PSA).

My first professional tournaments were a circuit of 3 events in New Zealand followed by 2 in Kenya. Of course Jonathan Kemp played these too. My Dad actually came with me to Nairobi. He had done some travelling with work and it had given him a sense of wanderlust and Kenya offered him an opportunity to visit somewhere slightly unusual. These tournaments went OK; I reached 4 Quarter-Finals and one Final, losing out in a final game tie-break after squandering a championship point. Gutted.

This was my life now; living in Sheffield at University and training every day. Flying to tournaments all over the world and playing two or three league matches every week (which I got paid for, so I was a relatively "rich" student – or at least until I had to spend all the money on flights to Brazil, Qatar, The USA etc) - oh and I would also attend the very occasional lecture (something my conscientious wife curses me for regularly!).

I loved playing the PSA circuit and climbed from 350 to 64 in the world in my first 2 years. Annoyingly at the age of 21 I had an inflamed disc in my lower back which needed physio and a few injections. This rehab set me back quite a few months and my ranking slipped down 20 places. After this I played another year of tournaments but the tedium of travelling started to hit me. I clearly remember one of my last tournaments. It was only an hour flight away in Holland. I was sitting at Manchester Airport waiting to board the plane and thinking to myself "I can't wait to come home" - That can't be good? How could I expect to perform well when I didn't even want to be there?

This was a big warning sign for me so I really began thinking what I was going to do about it. This feeling of indifference also coincided with University ending and living back at home in Bramhall (South Manchester). My Mum was becoming increasingly frustrated with me because she never saw the merit or potential in a squash career. I had also just met Helena, my absolutely perfect wife-to-be. My circumstances had changed and so had my focus.

I personally felt that at the age of 22 with the potential I had, I should be top 20 in the world by now (even after a slight injury time out). Over the years I've seen so many squash players who are happy to play the World Tour and linger around the 40's and 50's in the rankings for their whole professional career, which don't get me wrong is an amazing standard to achieve consistently, but certainly not for me. I was playing squash to be among the sport's absolute elite. If I was to be a top 5 player, or top 1, I felt I should be close to that ranking at 22 years old. This may be harsh as many people 'mature' later into their twenties and don't get near the top of the senior ranks until they are in their late twenties or early thirties (take Andy Murray for example; who at the age of 29 became the oldest tennis player to reach World No.1 for the first time). I wasn't willing to risk it. I did not want to be a financially poor squash player forever. I began to open my mind to the possibility of different career options. Then I recognized an opportunity right on my doorstep...

There was a great player and coach called Marcus Berrett who lived in Halifax (about an hour drive from Manchester). He was 29. For years he'd been playing many leagues in the UK, beating world top 20, and some top 10 players. He was obviously a fantastic squash player but generally underperformed when travelling to PSA events. His main role though was as a coach. He coached 'club players' as well as some professionals. He was making more money than anyone outside the world's top 10. At this time he was offered a coaching job in Milan and he took it. I saw this as opportunistic timing and an ideal role for me to slot in to - a player and a coach who could fill the void Marcus was about to leave. In my eyes this role was perfect for a charismatic young man like myself. I felt confident I had the discipline to do long stints of coaching, knowing it would often be boring. I had the playing standard to receive good money for any league matches I played. I knew this could be a career path for me because I'd be using all my best skills. Looking back, this was probably my first entrepreneurial decision.

With my decreasing desire to travel and play the world circuit, coupled with a great opportunity to coach and continue my playing, and also meeting Helena who I was sure could be my wife, I made the decision to retire from the PSA tour, even though I was only 22 years old and it was my dream to be squash World Champion.

The last PSA event I ever played was in Athens, Greece. I reached the final but unfortunately lost to a phenomenal player called Ramy Ashour, who was the world junior champion at the time and was now beginning to focus his attention to the senior tour. Currently he has won the senior World Championships 3 times. Annoyingly I lost the final after having a championship point in the final game. Crazy I finished my PSA Tour life in the same way it began, losing in a final. I approached this tournament completely differently to any competition I had ever played in the past. I treated the event more like a travelling tourist with a bit of compulsory squash thrown in. I wasn't concerned about sitting around the hotel room all day to conserve energy. I went out walking, visiting all the major attractions; The Parthenon, Temple Of Zeus, the fist ancient Olympic stadium etc. Importantly, I was enjoying myself and low and behold, I played better squash. Interesting hey? It was the old cliché that now the pressure was off slightly I could really perform the way I wanted to.

A REAL JOB – ALMOST

"You are not stuck where you are unless you decide to be."

WAYNE DYER

I soon found a club to coach at. Grove Park Squash, Cricket and Rugby Club was my local club, 2 minutes from where I lived. It's the club where I started playing with my Dad when I was 10. I wasn't paid a retainer but I could use the courts for free and charge whatever I liked to coach the members. I could also advertise my racket-restringing service. All in all, Grove Park was a decent club to begin my trade. I was playing league matches on Tuesday and Wednesday evenings, and also played in the Danish and German Leagues some weekends. Money was coming in at last, and even though I had stopped training (and never have since I ceased the PSA World Tour), I was playing great. I was beating players on a weekly basis who I struggled with when I was playing the tour.

As you can probably imagine from my slightly obsessive, all-in attitude - when I did train I used to train extremely hard. From the age of 16, I trained as intensely as I could for every session, 2 or 3 times a day, every day. I continued this until my last PSA event in Greece, then I simply stopped. The fact I was now on court 6, 7 or 8 hours a day coaching (I am an especially active coach) my fitness levels were being maintained, but my skill levels and understanding of the game were improving. Coupled with the fact I was slightly more relaxed on court, my squash actually improved! I'm the only professional squash player turned coach in history, who improved their squash after their international playing career was over, and all without training.

After 4 years I moved to another club, only 10 minutes away in a popular village called Didsbury. This was a great club for a young squash coach; it was nicer with more members who were generally wealthier, and the club paid me a monthly retainer. I stayed there for 8 years. In this time I got married and had 2 incredible daughters. Coaching demand increased every year as did my reputation. I started to coach professionals which is what I really wanted to do. I have always felt my strengths were more at the elite level, as I don't have the patience to coach beginners!

My playing level remained constant. I continued playing my league matches and also the UK circuit of tournaments. Even though it's the UK circuit, anyone of any nationality can enter, so several world ranked players residing in the UK would play every event, all the way up to world top 10 players. I loved the challenge of playing against these top guys ranked near the very top of the world standings. I'd usually lose but I'd score the occasional win. With 13 tournament victories, I am the all-time record holder for tournament victories. I had become the new Marcus Berrett!

Throughout the last 13 years people have often asked me why I retired from the PSA so early in my career. I tell them the story I have just told you, of waiting at the airport wishing I wasn't there and so on. I don't really care if other people agree with my choice to stop or not, I have never regretted the decision I made. It was calculated and the correct decision at the time. I enjoy my life very much.

I WANNA BE STARTIN' SOMETHIN'

"People often avoid making decisions out of fear of making a mistake. Actually the failure to make decisions is one of life's biggest mistakes."

NOAH WEINBERG

Now, at 36, I coach less. Recently I made the decision to focus on where my strengths and passions lie in terms of squash. I mainly coach professionals as I was losing motivation to coach 'Club Players'. I liked every single player I coached, and have had great relationships with all of those, and I still do, but coaching them was not what was making me happy. I still play one league match every week. This weekly match, along with coaching professional players, gives me just enough competition to satisfy my playing needs. I'm not sure if I would ever want to fully stop playing high intensity matches. It feels great to step on a squash court ready for battle. It gives you a buzz and a sweaty workout unlike any other sport or activity. Squash truly is a unique sport.

This new streamlined approach gives me scope to follow new passions away from the squash court and importantly more time for what's really important in my life; my wife and children.

I've always been a particularly present Dad which was the beauty of being self-employed. I could tailor my work around spending time with my daughters. I love my situation now because it gives me the evenings with my family instead of heading out to coach again after I've collected my girls from school as I used to do. **Self-improvement is about priorities. Knowing what is important to you and doing what you're best at.**

I have my own sports clothing brand called AWsome Sports. I wanted to inject more time and effort into that, which my new situation accounts for and I've seen a dramatic improvement in the business. It has been nice to see more time and effort results in more sales. As I said, this new career move has also allowed plenty of time for other projects. I have such a unique set of skills which I know can be extremely useful. I want to help people - so here I am; writing and starting something new and exciting.

"I didn't come this far, only to come this far."

ANON

3 FAIL TO PLAN, PLAN TO FAIL

"It takes as much energy to wish as it does to plan"

ELEANOR ROOSEVELT

My aim for this book is to dramatically increase or even kick start your professional development by focusing on the following areas: the importance of goal setting; the danger of your "Chimp Brain"; the never-to-be-underestimated role of good old fashioned effort; and the concept of 'deliberate practice'. All of these factors play a massive part in our success. All mean nothing however, if we are not pursuing the correct path for us. This is why it is important to realize the power of our very own strengths, how to identify them and how to develop a 'super-strength'.

Of course we will closely examine which route is best to follow for each of us and what decisions to make in order to succeed in our chosen careers… but before we get to that, the first step is to take a close look at the consequences of setting goals, and how this is an essential practice for anybody looking to progress their career.

No Goals = No Ambition

Know Goals = Know Ambition

DON'T SPECULATE – STATEGIZE

"A goal properly set is halfway reached"

ZIG ZIGLAR

Goal setting involves the development of an action plan designed to motivate and guide a person or group toward a goal.

From an early age, nobody achieves anything significant without first setting goals. These are not always conscious but they are always there. As we make our way through adulthood these goals need to become more conscious and targeted.

Clarity in business is of paramount importance. If we want to accomplish anything great in our professional careers we cannot overlook the value of personal goals.

Setting goals offers great psychological benefits:

Goals:
- Organize us
- Narrow and direct our attention
- Make us more efficient
- Aid self-belief
- Provide motivation even after possible setbacks
- Prevent procrastination
- Increase our effort levels

But without a doubt the two most powerful aspects of setting goals are:

- *GOALS CLARIFY OUR LONG TERM VISION*
- *GOALS MAKE US ACCOUNTABLE*

In this Chapter we will look at the value of setting goals and how it has worked for real people and how it *WILL* WORK FOR YOU TOO. We will specifically examine the two main points above; vision and accountability, and how those two factors can lead us to amazing developments in our lives.

MR MOTIVATOR

"Our goals can only be reached through a vehicle of a plan, in which we must fervently believe, and upon which we must vigorously act. There is no other route to success."

PABLO PICASSO

A study in the European Journal of Social Psychology found that people who are specific about their plans are considerably more likely to act on them. People who rely solely on mental resolutions have a 35% chance of success, whereas people who clearly state when and how they will act have a 91% success rate.

If we want to get the most out of ourselves or somebody else, there must be direction. Even the most naturally driven people will not push themselves to their limit if there is not a strong external urge to

do so. This is where a goal is absolutely essential.

After comprehensive research Locke and Latham concluded that it is not sufficient to simply urge employees to "do their best". "Doing one's best" has no external reference, which makes it useless in producing specifically driven behaviour. This results in poor performance.

To elicit some specific form of behaviour from any person (whether it is ourselves or somebody else), it is important that this person has a clear view of what is expected from him/her. The goal must be specifically set out and incentivized in some way. A goal is thereby fundamental to success because it helps an individual to focus his or her efforts in a specified direction.

Goals with an appropriate incentive have a direct correlation to personal motivation. Only motivated individuals will achieve their goal.

My junior squash days were extremely goal orientated without actually sitting down to plan what I wanted to achieve each year. I didn't really know anything about goal setting when I was 12 but I knew I wanted to get to the top of the England Junior Ranking List, and I knew I was willing to work damn hard to do it. My rivalry with Jonathan Kemp was a huge drive for me. Though in the bigger scheme of things, overtaking him was actually a mini-goal or 'stepping stone', which was only present as an obstacle to achieve my main goal - becoming the England junior No.1. At this time of my life, this was a slightly unconscious goal in the fact that my Dad and I had discussed it without specifically sitting down to form some kind of action plan. It was the drive inside me that gave me the unyielding motivation to see out my wish.

Once I was 16 I knew I wanted to go to the next level and be a professional squash player, so becoming one of the world's best became a greater goal than wanting to be England Junior No.1. The desire to become the best junior in England did not wane with the additional of the other goal, it merely became a 'stepping stone'. As I said, I did not ever actively plan these goals, they were just inside me. Looking back, was it too young to be consciously setting goals? Definitely not. I had just never been introduced to it. In fact, I was not introduced to goal setting until I was in my 30's. Which seems ridiculous now.

I have good friend and successful entrepreneur Lawrence Jones to thank for introducing me to the importance of goal setting. It's a shame he wasn't around for me 20 years ago!

I know I could have achieved so much more if I had begun consciously goal setting when I was 16, and continued the process every year. And if I regularly sat down to assess where I was on my desired pathway toward my goal. This is why I want to help others. I don't want people to miss out on their full potential. We are never too old to start this process.

Setting a goal doesn't guarantee success. We must commit to our goal. There's no doubt Effort = Reward. A goal in our head, made one day in a flight of fancy, and then left there with no action, will obviously not materialize. A goal which is written down, planned, processed, regularly addressed with updated progress reports is considerably more likely to happen - I'm sure everyone will agree. I wasn't aware of goal setting and the gravity it holds until my 30's. I want you to know what I wished I had known all those years ago. I have learned that it is never too late. I want to show everyone what I have experienced over the past 5 years and how quickly it can lead to great things - really great.

STEP 1: THE WRITING'S ON THE WALL

"People with clear, written goals, accomplish far more in a shorter period of time than people without them could ever imagine."

BRIAN TRACY

The importance of Goal Setting has come to prominence much more in the 21st century with the emergence of business and life enhancing "gurus"… and there is a reason for this; it works as a method to achieve sustained focus and drive. All leading businessmen and entrepreneurs do it, top athletes do it - anybody can goal set, and everybody should! First we must know the steps of how to set goals which we will achieve.

Step one of successful goal setting that we simply have to understand is the power of written goals (the key point to note here is the word "WRITTEN").

People who write down their goals are 42% more likely to achieve them than the ones who don't. Telling a friend increases this rate to 78%.

Writing a goal down makes it more physical. It shifts from an imaginary realm to become an accountable force which we must act upon. I realize using the word "force" sounds rather dramatic. Believe me though, writing down our goal does create a certain momentum. Momentum with accountability. Accountability is another factor which increases our chances of success.

By physically writing down our goal we create a potential in our own mind which will ensure we will see our goal through to the very end. Having written goals provides us with an internal motivation to achieve what we have set out to do. This 'force' grows even stronger when we widen the field of accountability, as we will see in the following study.

A well-documented study was conducted by psychology professor Dr Gail Matthews of the Dominican University Of California. She found that those who wrote down their goals accomplished significantly more than those who did not write down their goals.

- Here is the study:

149 participants completed this study. The participants ranged in age from 23 to 72, with 37 males and 112 females. Participants came from the United States, Belgium, England, India, Australia and Japan and included a variety of entrepreneurs, educators, healthcare professionals, artists, attorneys, bankers, marketers, human services providers, managers, vice presidents, directors of non-profits, etc.

Research Design:

Participants were randomly assigned to one of 5 conditions (groups):

Group 1 - Unwritten Goal;
Group 2 - Written Goal;
Group 3 - Written Goal & Action Commitments;
Group 4 - Written Goal, Action Commitments to a Friend;
Group 5 - Written Goal, Action Commitments & Progress Reports to a Friend.

• Participants in Group 1 were simply asked to think about their goals (what they wanted to accomplish over the next 4 weeks) and then asked to rate that goal on the following dimensions: Difficulty, Importance, the extent to which they had the Skills & Resources to accomplish the goal, their Commitment and Motivation to the goal, whether or not they had pursued this goal before and if so their Prior Success.

• Participants in Groups 2-5 were asked to write (type into the online survey) their goals and then to rate their goals on the same dimensions.

• Group 3 was also asked to formulate action commitments.

• Group 4 was asked to formulate action commitments and send their goals and action commitments to a supportive friend.

• Group 5 was asked to formulate action commitments and send their goals, action commitments and weekly progress reports to a supportive friend. Participants in this group were also sent weekly reminders to email quick progress reports to their friend.

At the end of 4 weeks participants were asked to rate their progress and the degree to which they had accomplished their goals.

Results:

1. *Types of goals:*
Participants pursued a variety of goals including (in order of frequency reported) completing a project, increasing income, increasing productivity, getting organized, enhancing performance/achievement, enhancing life balance, reducing work anxiety and learning a new skill.
Examples of "completing a project" included writing a chapter of a book, updating a website, listing and selling a house, completing a strategic plan, securing a contract, hiring employees and preventing a hostile take-over.

2. *Goal Achievement:*
Group 5 achieved significantly more than all the other groups; Group 4 achieved significantly more than Groups 3 and 1; Group 2 achieved significantly more than Group 1.

3. *Differences between all writing groups and the non-writing group:*
Although the previous analysis revealed that Group 2 (written goals) achieved significantly more than Group 1 (unwritten goals), additional

analysis were performed to determine whether there were also differences between the group that had not written their goals (Group 1) and all groups that had written their goals (Groups 2-5). This analysis revealed that the mean achievement score for Groups 2-5 combined was significantly higher than Group 1.

Conclusions:

- *The positive effect of accountability was supported*: those who sent weekly progress reports to their friend accomplished significantly more than those who had unwritten goals, wrote their goals, formulated action commitments or sent those action commitments to a friend.

- There was *support for the role of public commitment*: those who sent their commitments to a friend accomplished significantly more than those who wrote action commitments or did not write their goals.

- *THE POSITIVE EFFECT OF WRITTEN GOALS WAS SUPPORTED*: Those who wrote their goals accomplished significantly more than those who did not write their goals.

"With the proliferation of business and personal coaching and the often anecdotal reports of coaching success it is important that this growing profession be founded on sound scientific research."

"This study provides empirical evidence for the effectiveness of three coaching tools: accountability, commitment and writing down one's goals." *Dr Gail Matthews*

Pretty compelling evidence wouldn't you say? We all knew after reading the results what the conclusions were, it was obvious for all to see. What was fascinating though was the addition of including other people for accountability. **Thorough goal setting is a crucial step toward personal development – and the more people we involve, and in particular close friends or people we admire, the more chance we have of achieving our goals.**

1. *SET A GOAL*

2. *WRITE it down*
3. *TELL at least one person you respect and regularly encounter (accountability)*
4. *MONITOR progress at specific points along the journey*
5. *SUCCESS!*

STEP 2: GOING FOR GOALD

"A goal without a plan is just a wish."

ANTOINE DE SAINT-EXUPERY

When asked about personal goals, most people conjure up blurry targets for themselves, for example, make more money, get promoted, or start my own business. These goals are no good. We must understand how to set meaningful goals and the techniques required in order to achieve them. Professional goal setting gives us clarity.

Generally considered there are 4 steps which successful entrepreneurs use to create clear and measurable goals. If we follow them these steps will not only help us to set the right goals for ourselves but also make sure we remain focused and achieve them no matter how many obstacles we face or how long they take.

Here we go:

- *   *Create a Vision*

Close your eyes and try to picture what it is you want? What does it look like? What does it feel like? Do you already have skills that can help toward your ideal vision? Yes you do is the answer – we will examine what unique skills each of us have at length in the next Chapter. Don't be afraid to dream big.

- *Make It Measurable* (we've already seen the power of this with Dr Gail Matthew's study)

Now think of your goal and quickly write it down. Ask questions depending on the kind of goal you have set for yourself: Do you work for yourself; do you have an employer; or is it best to start off working with a company to gain experience and learn guided pathways? Here we want to be as detailed as possible. Choose an achievable time frame. Set yourself up for success by outlining smaller, more obviously achievable goals that will all be stepping-stones toward the larger, end goal.

- *Set Manageable Benchmarks*

Be willing to continually break down each stepping-stone, into even smaller goals. These are a great way to keep us motivated and on track. Be willing to adjust your stepping-stones slightly as you learn, but never lose sight of the end goal, just know what has to be done to reach it.

- *Celebrate your successes*

Congratulate yourself after each completed stepping-stone. Maybe a beer, a glass of wine or a nice take-away.

Don't forget why you want to achieve your end goal, and don't be afraid of thinking how you will celebrate once you get there. A Shopping spree? Time off? A holiday?

The absolute key points to be taken from these steps are:

- Create a goal which is right for you.
- Write it down (we know this).
- Set a realistic time frame.
- Break down your ultimate goal into smaller goals - stepping stones.
- Celebrate your mini-victories.
- Learn as you go.
- If needed, adjust your stepping stones but...... *NEVER LOSE SIGHT OF, OR COMPROMISE YOUR END GOAL*

MAKE THE IMPOSSIBLE POSSIBLE

"All who have accomplished great things have had a great aim, have fixed their gaze on a goal which was high, one which sometimes seemed impossible"

ORISON SWETT MARDEN

When starting out on a journey of self-improvement it can be hard to keep sight of the end result. It can be easy to become bogged down with the "what-ifs?" This is where our action plan comes into play. This action plan is paramount to keep us focused and on track, no matter what comes our way. We have chosen to set our goal for a reason – it's something we strongly desire. We must not allow ourselves to be deterred. Eyes on the prize at all times.

For you to do this regularly, visualize your end goal, and remind yourself of the manageable smaller steps you need to tick off in order to reach the end. Don't be afraid to think about how you will celebrate when you get there (champagne works for me!).

In order to achieve our goals we must stick to our four point action plan. Let me emphasize these points one more time:

    o   *Write it down.*

This is the one key point I want everyone to take away from this Chapter. **WRITE IT DOWN.** It turns our goal from mere fantasy with a 1% chance of follow-through, into a real driving force that we will act upon. Once we have set the right goal for us, committing it to paper or a whiteboard is the first step to achieving this goal. If we don't do this we might as well throw the towel in now.

    o   *Tell someone:*

Become accountable. We definitely will not want to fail now, especially in the eyes of a person who we respect and admire. Make reasons to see this person regularly. The more we see them, the more they will ask how we are progressing, and the less we will want to fail.

o *Break down your goal:*

Turn your goal into 'fast wins' with stepping stones. These make your goal seem more manageable and more achievable. It is not a 'cop-out' to do this. These smaller, easier goals are still building toward the greater goal, never forget that. They simply make the goal more manageable and less daunting. These stepping stones will give us stamina and will keep us focused until the very end.

o *Celebrate:*

Don't be afraid to celebrate even the smallest of victories. This will serve to keep us happy. A happy worker is a motivated worker. A motivated worker is a productive worker.

THE RIGHT GOAL FOR YOU

So, we now know how to set a goal but how do we set the right goal for us? Goals are useless if they are not relevant to us. Do you even know what career is best suited to you? Do you think you know, or do you have no idea whatsoever? Many of us do not know but the next Chapter will deal with this question head on, and could prove to be a big eye-opener for many of us.

No Goal = No Ambition

Know Goal = Know Ambition

"If you don't know where you are going, every road will get you nowhere"

HENRY KISSENGER

4 PLAY TO YOUR STRENGTHS

"True success lies in knowing your weaknesses and playing to your strengths."

SOPHIA AMORUSO

Here's a question everybody should ask themselves at the start of each year:

How will I make this year better than the last?

And what if I promised that you could increase your chances of success using the skills you already have? So everything you need to improve and succeed you already have. That would be great right?

For those of you who work for a company - do you have unused potential at work? If so, you are not alone; far from it. Research tells us at least 60% of employees feel they have "untapped potential". Society generally looks to highlight problems above rewarding successes. Too often we focus on our weaknesses instead of our strengths - so we are always playing catch up, while our strengths remain underused in a ready position.

The next Chapters contain information that will make it obvious what it is we all need to do, what changes we should make and what actions we need to take to really get the best out of ourselves. These Chapters will be the reason you choose this book over any other as the one resource to help instigate progress* in your life, and lead you to great success.

My firm belief is that *focusing on our strengths is the fastest, surest way to career success.*

*Note "progress" but not necessarily "change". It may involve change, possibly a drastic change, but it also may not. I want to help you realize how you will get the best out of yourself using your current skillset. This may lead you down a path of change; a change of career or just a change in your approach to certain tasks in your current form of employment. Whatever happens, progress is what will be achieved. Progress leads to success.

SELF-HELP OR THE LACK OF...

"Do what makes you feel good. Remind yourself of what you're good at and make sure you do that."

JESSIE J

Far too often I see people focusing on their weaknesses. There are countless 'self-help' books which say that in order to improve oneself or achieve greatness we should constantly analyze ourselves to highlight what we're bad at, and then look to correct these. People are always looking for a quick fix; a book to read or a course to go on that will eradicate their perceived weaknesses and all will be right with their life.

There are also thousands of books and programmes that show us a specific path to take for enlightenment or self-improvement. They state the method they have is the one genius theory that if we follow it to the letter we'll achieve great wealth. One path cures all. Nonsense.

Don't even get me started on the number of exercise or dieting books!

All these 'self-help' programs that suggest their way is the best; they use lines like "new science shows us…" or "results like these have never before been achieved… until now". Usually they do not have anything unique but are endorsed by some 'celebrity' to lure people in. They prey upon people's desire for a quick fix, and for something new to excite them. These books are all trying to show us that their method is the ultimate way and that they have a genuine USP (Unique Selling Point); but we all know they've simply rebranded another weak idea, or it's simply a fad. A fad which people follow just for another one to come along a year later, and so on and so on.

The successful books that stand the test of time are more inspirational and motivational based studies. Genuine studies not theories (which is not always easy to spot the difference). They are the ones which try to inject enthusiasm and a lust for life into their audience. Not telling them what to do, but instead offering guidance to a path which is right for them as an individual. Not offering a quick fix but inspiring them on a journey of self-discovery (as outrageously cheesy as I know that sounds!). It is these authors/speakers which have a higher success rates of producing longer lasting effects. Every one of us is different, and this must be acknowledged.

EVERYONE HAS A USP

"From now on – specialize; never again make any concession to the ninety-nine percent of you which is like everyone else at the expense of the one percent which is unique."

CYRIL CONNOLLY

Every person is unique. Everybody's accumulative beliefs, ideas, attitudes and physical characteristics can never be the same - all amalgamating to make each person have a totally unique personality and set of skills. Each person on this planet therefore has their own USP. Even if we don't believe there is anything special about us, we must recognize that we are different to any other human on this earth, therefore we have potential to succeed in a way which only we are capable of. The difficultly is finding our way.

Most commonly a USP is why people should choose one particular product over another product; or choose one brand over another brand; or choose one person over another person. Effective branded advertising achieves this. It explains why their product or brand is the best choice for us as the consumer. As a unique individual with a potentially great professional career ahead of us, we need to find a way to market ourselves, and to stand out from the crowd. It is not just products that require marketing, it is people too if we want to stand out from a crowd.

Now don't worry, marketing does not have to be brash and 'in your face'. It can be subtle, more of a slow-burn. Quietly demonstrating our skills and successes achieves this. We're talking about self-marketing.

A sportsman needs to showcase his/her best attributes in order to win. If you work for a company, or are selling a product or service, you need to highlight your benefits. You have to show that what you offer or what you produce is meaningful. It's all about presenting yourself as indispensable to your bosses or your customers.

We must all remember we are unique, and we CAN differentiate ourselves from others.

At the beginning of this Chapter we saw that 60% of us feel we have "untapped potential" which is not utilized in our jobs. Research also shows that over 80% of us say we are not choosing to hide our true worth, but it is more the case that our employer simply doesn't ask or delve deep enough to find it. This is a somewhat pathetic excuse. The assumption should not be for our employer or even our coach to find out what strengths we have to offer. We cannot expect that other people will discover our true worth, we must show them if we are to achieve the success we are all individually capable of. The onus solely falls upon our shoulders to showcase what we can do. We need to take responsibility for our own progress (or lack of). No excuses.

INFERIORITY COMPLEX ANYONE?

"Blaming others for your problems is like blaming donuts for being fat. It wasn't the donut, it was the choice."

JEFF GITMOR

Be confident. Too many days are wasted comparing ourselves to others and wishing to be something we aren't. Everybody has their own strengths and weaknesses, and it is only when we accept everything we are - and aren't - that we will truly succeed.

Everybody feels inferior in some way or another, and the reason for this is we do not accept that everybody is unique. If everybody accepts they are totally unique, then there is no question of inferiority. Everybody is just one of a kind; so comparison should not arise.

This is considerably easier said than done, and is probably an overly simplistic viewpoint. Some might even say it is human nature to compare. I would say it is possibly human nature to judge, which itself is a form of comparison. To judge sounds negative and often nasty, but my experience is that people are usually judging themselves in the negative way, not the other person. The reason for this is that every person, although unique, is similar enough in many aspects which causes the temptation to compare.

These self-judgements are our Chimp Brain putting us down. If we know what it is that makes us unique, and we truly embrace it, then we will not feel the need to make these comparisons. If we can do this then inferiority disappears.

"Personality begins where comparison ends." - KARL LAGERFELD

We need to identify what it is that makes us unique. Know what our strengths are. The more we know about ourselves, the less like anyone else we become.

Embrace who you are. But how?

Surely to counteract the feeling of inferiority we need to build our confidence?

The first step to improving our confidence is to understand how a lack-of-confidence affects us. Ask yourself what situations in life do you feel this lack-of-confidence and how does it reflect in your mood and your performance. In these situations, you will undoubtedly see a negative effect on your frame of mind which will in turn impact on your ability to perform at a high level, whether that is socially or professionally.

Do not worry though as it would be extremely rare for a person to feel unconfident in every area of their life, just as it would be equally rare for a person to feel confident in every aspect of their life. Just like it would also be impossible for somebody to perform perfectly or make the right decisions in every situation all of the time.

"To err is human." - *ALEXANDER POPE*

Now, identify which areas or situations make you feel self-assured or knowledgeable. Do not just look at location, but also at particular actions. These actions could be voluntary or involuntary. They may happen regularly or just occasionally. Whatever conditions you highlight, try to break these down into the most specific areas possible. The more exact you can be then the better your understanding of yourself will become:

Are you great in a crowd or better in a one-to-one situation? Are you a shy and reluctant teacher or do you perk up when someone wants to hear your opinion? Are you more relaxed in certain buildings that others? And so on...

So; we must know our positive and negative triggers. Embrace positive situations which give us a feeling of high self-worth. Positive situations will cause us to feel this way because they encourage our preferred personality traits and/or our areas of expertise. Who doesn't want to feel knowledgeable or to be considered one of the best?

This Chapter is about pinpointing areas of confidence and using our specific strengths in order to thrive and increase productivity.

BE THE ARTIST NOT THE PAINT

"I dream my painting, and then I paint my dream."

VINCENT VAN GOGH

I am a firm believer in playing to our strengths. Not focusing our attention on what we're weak at but in fact, identifying our unique strengths. What is it that makes you individual? What attributes do you possess that make you great, or at least, potentially great? We are all individual and we can all be exceptional.

Do not follow a certain path just because it worked for someone else. I'm not saying we should not have role models or people we admire, and I'm not saying not to use another person's achievements as a target to aspire to. It is definitely useful to find a mentor or a person of inspiration who has experienced a similar journey to us or the journey we would like to take. I know I've had several role models I've looked up to for inspiration throughout my life, often having several at the same time. But remember, our progress can be similar to theirs but it will not be exactly the same. **We are special and our route will need to be tailored to our own requirements, our own traits and our own strengths.**

It makes so much more sense to start out on any adventure by examining what we are good at (particularly in business). These can be personality strengths or skills we already possess. These might cover a range of activities or physical skill traits. They might include specific prowess we have already worked on and developed in a particular field, or maybe just a natural favouring of certain skills and tasks.

I hope you can see it is best to do what you are already accomplished at in order to succeed? The last thing we want to do is try to be somebody or something we are not. Just because a certain direction worked for one other person doesn't mean it's the right one for us. Personal achievement is specific to the individual, hence why it is *personal* achievement – it's their own vision and goals as set out by them. Your path to success will be driven by your vision and your goals, set out by you; paying close attention to your desires and all planned around your strengths.

There is rarely just one way to approach a task. We can make our own method using the solid attributes and skills we have as individuals. It may be longer at first, but it will be comfortable. Confidence will increase and it will reinforce our desire to get results. With time and through practice we will pick up other skills around our strengths which will serve to make us even more productive and successful.

Always apply what you know first.

CONQUERING CONFIDENCE

"Self-confidence is the first requisite to great undertakings."

SAMUEL JOHNSON

Confidence is one of the biggest issues human beings seem to have. A lack of confidence can come from making too many negative comparisons leading to an inferiority complex as discussed earlier in this Chapter. It most often provokes the feeling of 'not being good enough'. If we play to our strengths, it reinforces self-worth because we are doing the things we know we are good at; it makes us feel good. Everybody in the world likes to feel they are good at what they do. If we are good at what we do we will succeed more often, which further reinforces our successful actions and then we will be well on our way to conquering confidence.

People who play to their strengths at work are:

- Happier

- More Confident

- Have a higher self-esteem

- Have higher energy levels

- Less Stressed

- More resilient

- Nicer and more willing to help others

- More engaged

- More likely to achieve their goals

Overall these people perform considerably better.

A person using their strengths every day (in or out of the work environment):

- Exhibits lost sense of time (in a good way! They find themselves 'in the zone')

- Has rapid learning of new skills (we'll address this later in the book)

- Repeats pattern of success

- Always finish their task

- Yearns to apply their strengths

- Speaks clearly and enthusiastically

- Appears happy and optimistic

- Responds immediately to questions

- Enjoys a challenge

The above are all wonderful qualities that I'm sure you'd like to display every day, anyone would. If you did you would be more productive and more successful, and importantly the above are attributes that will make you a happier person.

In contrast, a person who does not apply their strengths:

- Struggles to express themselves

- Are hesitant to talk about work

- Focuses on problems instead of solutions

- Sounds dejected and flat

- Are more critical and unforgiving of themselves

- Looks to withdraw from a situation

- Appears disengaged

- Displays drooped posture

- Shows poor eye contact when in conversations.

Obviously the above are not good qualities to exhibit, and certainly not elements that would set us out to be a high achiever in life. *Do you do any of these?*

You've purchased this book so I can safely assume that you want to be a go-getter. You want to succeed. You want to be recognized. You want to be happy. So you must focus on what you're good at. You're an individual with your own qualities, your own strengths, your own set of skills, and it is these which will make you happy and successful.

"Low self-confidence isn't a life sentence. Self-confidence can be learned, practiced and mastered – just like any other skill. Once you master it, everything in your life will change for the better."

BARRIE DAVENPORT

STACK THE DECK IN YOUR FAVOUR

~

HOW TO IDENTIFY STRENGTHS

"Someone creates a trick, many people perfect it, but its final success in front of an audience depends on the person who presents it."

RENE LAVAND

Natural strengths are unique combinations of our physical attributes, human instincts, basic knowledge and basic skills that every person on earth possesses. Strengths can be further enhanced by including specific physical traits, personality strengths, acquired knowledge and learned skills. When asked, most people do not know what their real strengths are. They have never allowed themselves time to consider what it is that is good about themselves; what they are adept at, whether it be a personality or physical trait or skill. If you do not know what your strengths are, like most of the population, it's very rare to be regularly given the opportunity to use them. It's up to us to use and demonstrate our strengths. We cannot hope someone will recognize our strengths for us and give us a 'big break' out of nowhere.

In our childhood these were clearer because our strengths would guide us toward activities and subjects that fit our natural inclinations, or sparked our inner curiosity. In adulthood this intrinsic force fades, which can lead us down a path of indifference. We often become disconnected from our innate qualities. As we grow up we must work to stay connected with our natural strengths. The beauty is that when we do, as an adult we have the mental aptitude to apply, utilize and greatly improve these preferred characteristics.

Our strengths can be applied to anything, we just need to know what they are and rethink our strategy.

CLIFTON STRENGTHS FINDER

One of the few books which focuses on our individual strengths in order to achieve success is an American publication from 2001 called 'Now, Discover Your Strengths' by Marcus Buckingham and Donald Clifton. The theory behind the book is that each individual adult possesses a certain number of fixed universal personal-character attributes, which together result in an individual's tendency to develop certain skills more easily and excel in certain fields.

This book became well known as it was linked to an online personality assessment called 'Clifton's Strength Finder'.

This test defines 34 areas, what they call 'Talent Themes' that best describe the range of human uniqueness. Talents are people's naturally recurring patterns of thought, feeling, or behaviour. These are:

- Achiever - one with stamina and hard work, a constant drive for accomplishing tasks.

- Activator - one who starts things in motion, turns thoughts into action. Often impatient.

- Adaptability - one who will 'go with the flow'; Accommodating to changes in direction/plan.

- Analytical - one who requires data/proof to make sense of their circumstances. Analytical.

- Arranger - one who enjoys orchestrating many tasks and variables to a successful outcome.

- Belief - one who has certain core values; Strives to find some purpose for everything they do.

- Command - one who takes control; Steps up to positions of leadership.

- Communication - one who uses words to inspire action and education.

- Competition - one who thrives on comparison and competition to be successful. Desire to win.

- Connectedness - one who defies coincidences; Seeks to unite others through commonality.

- Consistency/Fairness - one who believes in treating everyone the same to avoid unfair advantage. Like to make and adhere to rules for all.

- Context - one who is able to use the past to make better decisions in the present. Historians.

- Deliberative - one who proceeds with caution, seeking to always have a plan. Anticipate obstacles.

- Developer - one who sees the untapped potential in others.

- Discipline - one who seeks to impose order to make sense of the world.

- Empathy - one who is especially in tune with the emotions of others.

- Focus - one who requires a clear sense of direction to be successful. They prioritize, then act.

- Futuristic - one who is inspired by the future and what could be. A visionary.

- Harmony - one who seeks to avoid conflict through consensus of agreement.

- Ideation - one who is adept at seeing underlying concepts in order to find connections.

- Includer - one who instinctively works to include everyone; Accepting of others.

- Individualization - one who uses the uniqueness of individuals to create successful teams.

- Input - one who is constantly collecting information or objects for future use. Crave knowledge.

- Intellection - one who enjoys thinking and thought-provoking conversation. Introspective.

- Learner - one who has a desire to constantly improve. Process of learning, rather than the outcome, is what excites them.

- Maximizer - one who seeks to take people and projects from great to excellent.

- Positivity - one who has a knack for bringing excitement to any situation. Contagiously enthusiastic.

- Relator - one who is most comfortable with fewer, deeper relationships. Like to work with friends.

- Responsibility - one who must follow through on commitments. Honest and loyal.

- Restorative - one who thrives on solving difficult problems.

- Self-Assurance - one who stays true to their beliefs, judgments and is confident of his/her ability.

- Significance - one who seeks to be seen as significant by others.

- Strategic - one who is able to see a clear direction through the complexity of a situation.

- Woo - one who is able to easily persuade. Love to 'break the ice'.

The test involves a number of generic questions: After completing all the required field of the online assessment, the program would provide the test-taker with their top five themes.

AN ACHIEVER BELIEVER

~

MY ANALYSIS OF THE CLIFTON STRENGTHS FINDER

"Some people dream of success… while others wake up and work hard for it."
MARK ZUCKERBERG

It is extremely important to know our personality strengths. Reading through the 'Talent Themes' I'm sure everyone will agree that these seem like accurate descriptions and are present characteristics in humans. We will all know people who strongly display certain 'Talents Themes' over others, and these particular traits can without a doubt be turned into strengths. I do agree with these 'themes'. I believe one of these characteristics needs to carry more weight than others, and it needs to be mentioned that without this one trait, great success will be impossible. That trait is the 'Achiever'.

THE ACHIEVER

Let's look at the full definition of The Achiever: *A person with a great deal of stamina and hard work, a constant drive for accomplishing tasks. They take great satisfaction from being busy and productive.*

So basically this is a person who would be described as motivated or completely dedicated. They are driven by self-improvement and job completion. Dedicated to their task in order to achieve their objective – they are completely goal driven.

I'm sure we can all agree without this, no one is going to achieve anything substantial (hence its name – the 'Achiever'!), and let me tell you, it's rarer than you might think. It is actually exciting to find a person who strongly displays this personality trait and commits to tasks to the extent required in order to be the best at something. From my experience these people stand out from the crowd; and why do they stand out from the crowd? Because not many have it.

One must not interpret that for an individual to be this dedicated they must be so single-minded that they don't have time to lead a normal life, or to be a nice human-being. I'm sure nobody would consider Roger Federer to be a bad person, far from it, he's a true gent; yet he has had to be selectively single-minded and dedicated to his chosen career, to such a degree that most 'normal' people couldn't even comprehend it.

In fact business leader Lawrence Jones has recently done a series of podcasts interviewing entrepreneurs covering a range of ages and business sectors, and speaking to him about these interviews his findings were interesting. He said the one common message to come out of these interviews; the one thing they all said was - to be a nice person and to be kind is the number one rule in business today. Surprised? Lawrence was surprised, but also delighted. It says great things about today's successful individuals. They live by their morals. Business has changed for the better from the 'dog-eat-dog' world of the 70's, 80's and 90's. We are currently in a more humane time, which almost seems a contradiction as we stand on the cusp of a more robotic workplace with the advances in Artificial Intelligence, computer technology and the emergence of 3D printers among other things. Achievers should not be cold robots, they should be nice people!

To be an 'Achiever' yet appear human is skill of life balance. What it takes is for a person to commit 100% to their goals but able to remain mentally present for others during the 'rest' periods. The skill to separate work from play (even though rest will still often involve tremendous discipline, particularly for a sportsman). This separation of work and rest is paramount for success (staying true to our values while remaining fresh for our brain and body to flourish).

WHIPP'S "TIERED TALENTS"

I have highlighted The Achiever trait as totally crucial. When it comes to the remaining 33 'Talent Themes', they should be ordered in a tiered pyramid, with the top being most important for entrepreneurial success. There should be 4 tiers, each tier is a rank of importance.

Tier 1: The Essential – The Achiever

Tier 2: Commitment (to achieving goals) – Belief, Competition, Focus and The Maximizer.

Tier 3: Feedback – Context, Input, Learner and Self-Assurance

Tier 4: Management – the remaining 25 themes.

To break this down;

- ## TIER 1: THE ESSENTIAL

The Achiever. We know about the importance of this. It is the unconditional, must-have theme for leaders, entrepreneurs or top sportsmen and women.

- ## TIER 2: COMMITMENT TO ACHIEVING GOALS

Belief - People strong in Belief have certain core-values that are unchanging. Out of these values emerges a purpose. We must believe that what we are doing is the best path to take. This belief will give us confidence and the will power to achieve what we have set out to achieve. We must stay true to ourselves. "Believe and you will succeed."

Competition – The best definition of this theme is 'a desire to be the best'.

Focus – These people follow-through and will make any corrections necessary to stay on track. They prioritize and act. They are willing to make changes to their method but never willing to change their goal.

Maximizer – A Maximizer looks to transform something strong into something superb. This is the perfect personality trait to give rise to super-strengths! (We'll come to these in Chapter 5). These are the innovators, the dreamers.

- ## TIER 3: FEEDBACK

Context – They understand the journey of what has happened in order to improve their present situation. Provide analysis and feedback.

Input – People strong here have a craving to know more. The constant researcher and analyzer. They thrive on information.

Learner – Learners have a great desire to gain knowledge because they want to continuously improve. I would look to disagree with the part of the official description that people strong in this field get excitement from the learning process rather than the outcome. I truly believe there are topic purists and people driven by outcome, but there definitely needs to be strong elements of both, even if one is stronger. If one is an idealist and driven by the process of learning and the aesthetic nature of what they are undertaking, then a successful outcome is a good indicator of that. And likewise vice versa; if one is completely results driven, they will not get the desired outcome without a satisfactory level of good technical application, even if it's not perfect. Roger Federer and Rafael Nadal would be a good example of this. Federer the purist, and Nadal the outcome competitor; but both want to set records and win titles.

Self-Assurance – Exactly what we have previously mentioned about self-confidence. These people are sure of their strengths and abilities and will continue even after a set-back. Similar to the Belief theme. However Belief is very much linked to focus on the task ahead, whereas this theme is centralized around confidence in oneself.

- TIER 4: MANAGEMENT

The remaining 'Talent Themes' I would consider to be the day to day management skills. Here lies the recognition of ones strengths.

They provide the individual with a method of choice. These 'themes' are not essential for success on their own, but direct how a person prefers to tackle their assignments. Through their day to day approach toward tasks, these traits shape how to perform best in order to achieve each mini goal.

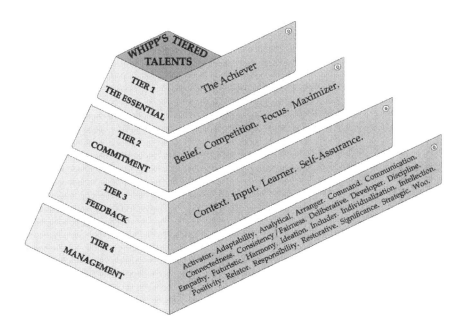

I firmly believe that a person who can truly set goals with the intention of becoming a success in their chosen field of activity, needs to have the following - to be an Achiever (Tier 1), to have a strong two traits from Tier 2, and another two from Tier 3. They need to recognize which two or three Tier 4 traits they display the strongest. These Tier 4 traits are how they should approach their daily tasks. These are the traits which will allow the individual to "play to their strengths".

Outlined above are the minimum requirements, however I would generally expect an Achiever type personality to have all of the Tier 2 traits, and probably all the Tier 3 traits too (although it is not essential for these Tier 3 traits to be strong, or even all present at first. They are feedback traits and they can be learned). If one has chosen the correct path and set suitable goals, then these Tier 3 traits will strengthen with enjoyment, and confidence.

People will naturally have many Tier 4 strengths. There is no right or wrong answer here. What's required is to simply pinpoint a few themes you relate to the most and look to utilize them. The important message here is to set about achieving your goals in the most efficient, the most productive, and the most enjoyable way for you. Never feel guilty to find a more enjoyable way of approaching jobs. If a person truly plays to their strengths they will enjoy their work much more. They will perform significantly better and have a much greater chance of success.

LET'S GET PHYSICAL

"The more you know yourself, the more clarity there is."
JIDDU KRISHNAMURTI

Surely to completely define ones strengths we need to not only look at personality characteristics, but physical ones too?

To get the most accurate assessment of a person, we also need to assess the individual's physical appearance and skill levels, as specific or specialized as they may be. Unfortunately there cannot be a generic test for this. It has to be a subjective appraisal by an appropriate coach or expert in that field. These results (along with their personality analysis) must be taken into account when defining all that a candidate has to offer.

Therefore it cannot be the case that to accurately identify all of a candidates strengths in terms of future prospects that there is simply an online test.

A person's main strengths may be; just a personality trait; or just a physical trait; or just a skill which has already been developed (which shows potential mastery). Much more likely, the worthiness of a candidates strengths will be a combination of at least two of these three areas.

So to summarize - in order to expertly assess a person's strengths not only requires a standard generic interview process and/or a personality test, but importantly must include specific task orientated observation and performance analysis carried out by an expert.

WHAT ARE *YOUR* STRENGTHS?

"Don't push your weaknesses, play with your strengths."

JENNIFER LOPEZ

Big question - *How is all this information relevant to you?* How can you apply what you've read so far and decide what *your* best characteristics are?

I hope you have already pinpointed certain 'Talent Themes' that best describe you. The tiered pyramid will give you an indication of what type of person you are. Don't worry if you feel you do not possess the Achiever trait to such an extent you could take over the world. Not everyone has to be a world leader, a world champion tennis player or an industrial pioneer. As we have discussed, people are different and it would be a boring planet if we all were not. As previously mentioned, the information in this book is relevant whether; you are a teenager at school; you are already in a particular line of work; you already have certain developed skills or you do not; you see yourself as an potential entrepreneur; maybe you are happy working where you are but want to perform better; or you are looking for a future career and have no idea what that may be.

Firstly though, before you begin deciding your Tier 4 personality strengths, you need to assess if you have any physical skills that you feel are above average. These could be a general sporting trait like speed, agility or endurance; or possibly a more specific prowess in a chosen activity like a soccer free-kick, the tennis serve, or as a baseball pitcher. Your physical skill can also be something less obviously 'physical' like computer programming, joinery, arts and craft; and again these can be further specialized if you already have your chosen field. This list has endless possibilities.

Remember; your strengths will show up to some extent everywhere you go and in everything you do – at home, work, and in leisure activities. For example, if you like to organize, you will probably find yourself organizing everything in your life; your desk, wardrobe, kitchen and even other people close to you. This would suggest you have a strong Discipline trait.

A great place to start is by asking yourself these questions:
What activities have you enjoyed the most since you were a child?
What is your most significant accomplishment to date?
What activities engage your attention?

What would you find easiest to teach to others?

If you decide that there is a skill you possess which you enjoy, and is of a high level and you feel it can be further improved and used as a base for your professional development, then move on to the next set of questions.

How does this strength(s) add value? Does it/ do they help you or others?

Do you currently enjoy doing this skill? Enjoyment is key.

Do you see the merit in using this skill? … If you don't then no one else will.

Is there a demand? No matter how niche that may be.

Do you feel you could possibly have a career which revolves around this skill? To do so you would have to be passionate enough about it, or at least passionate about the outcome it could give you.

If you have answered "yes" to the above questions, now is the time to examine if your physical traits are suitable. Does this skill have a particular physical requirement? eg. Basketball, or a soccer goalkeeper generally requires a minimum height in order to excel. Most things in life do not have such physical appearance pre-requisites for success, but it's worth checking.

If you are still on track with the above then that's great, time to move on to see if you have the mental attributes to see it through. This is where you scrutinize your 'talents' - and I mean really sit down and think if you do have the personality to apply yourself fully and see it through to the end. Do you have a combination of all which you need to pursue a self-employed career as a solo-artist? If you do not please do not fear at all, most people do not; most people are not solo-artists.

NOT AN ACHIEVER OR SOLO-ARTIST?

"Action separates the heroes from the cowards, the achievers from the complainers, the successful from the mere dreamers, the happy from the envious; it separates those who rise to the challenge of their goals from the haters who cower in the shadow of stagnancy."

Dr STEVE MARABOLI

Time to examine your personality by reading the 'Talent Themes' and consulting the pyramid. You must be completely honest with yourself, you don't want to kid yourself. If you do not choose honestly then you might follow a path that is wrong for you, and you will fail, so all you will have achieved is wasting yours, and possibly others time too. Do not consider yourself an Achiever, or a Maximizer if you are not. Most people are best suited to stand out as a top performer while working for a company in an office. There is nothing wrong with that at all. It is safe and offers security, mentally and financially. If you perform very well there is always scope for more. More opportunity, more money, and more challenge. You must know how to best tackle your job in relation to your strengths. This way you can achieve the best possible results - and impressive performances will always be rewarded.

OK, so you're not an Achiever type personality so the Tier 4 'Talent Themes' are the ones for you. Consult these again. This is your method. This is how you will excel at your assigned tasks. Tomorrow is a new day. Think how you can apply your strengths to any task or challenge you may currently have. Take a fresh approach and don't be afraid to go against convention. You can achieve anything if you stay true to what you're good at. Decide what your best methods are based on your personality strengths and apply them. Playing to your strengths will make you a happier, more confident worker. **A happy, confident worker is a productive worker.**

Then work up the pyramid - see if you possess any of the Tier 3 Talents, and remember these can also be learned. These will give you scope for improvement and skill acquisition.

CASE STUDIES

"I'm a very positive thinker, and I think that is what helps me the most in difficult moments."

ROGER FEDERER

Here are just a few cases of how focusing on strengths has helped these people massively. They allowed their strengths to dictate their goals and shape their pathway to success.

Rafael Nadal was seen as a clay-court specialist early in his career. His patience and endurance for base-line rallying was phenomenal. He was relentless. Even at 18 years old he was able to beat all the best players in the world, on clay! Then he was able to beat them on a hard surface because the tactical cross-over was very similar. It was assumed however, that there was no way he could beat Roger Federer on a grass court as the tactics and technical skills were too different due to the speed of the ball coming of the surface. Grass court tennis had always required a fast serve and competent volleying, Nadal was famed for neither.

Suddenly he started to do well at Wimbledon, reaching the final in 2006 and 2007, still people thought there was no way he could ever win it. Nadal didn't change his style of game to the conventional grass-court style, even though everyone was saying he should. What Nadal did have was excellent defensive skills and tenacity. He shortened his backswing slightly to cope with the faster and lower bouncing ball. He used these skills to become one of the most consistent returners of serve the game has ever seen. He could get the fast grass-court serve back over the net, when others couldn't. Once he was in the rally, he could continue to hustle and lure his opponents into a base-line rally. Now they were playing his style of game.

Nadal did win Wimbledon (twice). The first time in 2008 beating his rival Federer in one of the most memorable matches of all time. Nadal stuck to what he was good at. He had to adapt slightly to the faster surface with the use of a shorter backswing and flatter ground strokes as opposed to his heavy top spin forehands on clay courts; but he never changed his approach. He stayed true to his attritional strengths and completely defied common opinion of how to win on a grass-court. He went against a 100 year old theory and won!

Lawrence Jones is the founder and CEO of UKFast. I mentioned him in the last Chapter in regards to Goal Setting. UKFast is currently one of the fastest growing companies year on year in England. Lawrence is also in the UK Top 20 Entrepreneurs list.

Lawrence believes his success is largely down to his goal setting. Achieving manageable targets in order to realize much greater goals. He has a natural drive and commitment. I would consider his main 'Talent' traits to be; Achiever, Command, Competition, Futuristic, Maximizer, Self-Assurance and Strategic. Note he has The Achiever, Competition and Maximizer traits. Coupled with his Self-Assurance, these all make for a dynamic combination.

This innate aspirational quality in him intensified after he was caught in a near fatal avalanche in his twenties. He was buried under snow for 8 minutes. He had passed out and presumed himself to be dead.

Since that near-fateful day in February 2001, he has been determined to get as much out of life as possible. He values time. Time to work and time to rest. This is where his goal setting is of incredible importance. Everything has a time frame. He values feedback in order to improve; another important feature of achieving ones goals.

However, I personally believe it is not his goal setting which sets him apart from other high achieving businessmen. Goal setting is an essential practice in order to achieve great things, but it is not uncommon. Knowing Lawrence as well as I do, I see his strength as something much more unique. He has a 'dare to be different' attitude. Pair this with his love of facts and often childishly stubborn personality, he has the confidence to be individual and sometimes outrageous.

He is a big advocate in hiring women as well as men. Sadly, common perception of I.T. would not immediately include so many women in the office. He would employ strong-willed women who were happy to compete in a (generally considered) male environment. The women would thrive on the competition. Their presence would kick-start a primal instinct in the men which would also make the men work considerably harder, increasing output and performance. Genius! There cannot be many businessmen who would be willing to set up their first big office in this way.

His emphasis has always been that staff come first. Obviously you need to deliver the best service possible for your customers, especially when you are a tech company and competition is high, but if you look after your staff they will look after your customers for you. His idea is to offer a more personal, caring service. He does this with his staff and his customers. Lawrence regularly rewards and treats his staff who perform well. They feel happy and valued, so they come to work feeling positive every day, which in turn is reflected in their performance. Happy staff = Happy customers.

He regularly takes staff to Snowdon (the highest peak in Wales) for the weekend, or more recently Verbier in the Swiss Alps, for fun challenges and chill out time. The staff bond together as a team and they come away with a feeling of importance and value. And in-turn, they come back to Manchester and deliver an outstanding performance at work, which they feel good about and of course it earns more money for UKFast, and therefore Lawrence. Performing well also increases their chances of being noticed as a high achiever which will lead to recognition, hopefully for them in the shape of a bonus or a promotion.

The UKFast Head Office is more like a playground than what we would perceive as an office. There are chill out areas, sleep pods, a gym and games. Staff are encouraged to work in intense bursts then relax, recover and start again, as opposed to a boring 9.00 to 5.00 medium-paced slog. The whole building is geared toward inspiration and getting the most out of his workforce.

Obviously Lawrence has very developed technical skills too and there is no doubt that his emphasis on goals is vital to his success; Goal Setting is his management system. It controls him. But it is his "dare to be different" attitude which sets him apart from 99% of other business owners. It regularly generates him and his company positive press coverage, but most importantly this approach is the reason UKFast offer exceptional service and sets them apart from their competition.

I like these two examples because they both started out targeting different personal strengths. One had physical strengths, and the other personality.

Nadal was already aware he was a good athlete before he knew his long-term focus would be to pursue a life playing professional tennis. His environment allowed him the opportunity to play tennis. By environment I mean he had local access to a tennis club with coaching available. Nadal's uncle was a former professional tennis player. As his passion and ability in tennis grew, his family were willing to sacrifice even more of their time and money to help him further improve as it became obvious he was an excellent junior tennis player and an exceptional athlete. His career choice was originally derived from his impressive physical abilities. He had a strong urge toward sport as it suited his strengths. As previously mentioned in this chapter, he also had a strong Achiever personality trait too. This combination of strengths, coupled with his environment made it possible for Rafael to choose professional tennis, and to go on to become one of the greatest tennis players of all time. Currently he's won 16 Grand Slam titles, second only to Roger Federer who is on 19.

Lawrence actually moved to Manchester from North Wales and begun his career as a pianist when he was in his early twenties. He was (and still is) excellent on the piano. So good, he thought he could possibly have forged a career in music. He knew the music industry and realized there were too many factors out of his control in order to achieve the kind of success he desired. He knew though that he had personality characteristics that would be well suited to business, so he took the leap of faith and backed himself to start up a website hosting company as he saw a gap in the market. He's a visionary and opportunist. His success was borne from specific personality strengths.

One more example I'd like to mention:

As a junior soccer player, I was a decent goalkeeper. Due to my lack of height I was unable to impose myself in a crowded penalty area. I had to prove my worth in other areas in my particularly specialized position. I was considerably more athletic than the average goalkeeper. I had great reactions and agility, which was shown in my shot-stopping ability. I also became known as a penalty saving expert.

If you don't know, a penalty kick in soccer is where the attacker has a free shot at goal with just the goalkeeper to beat. The average score rate is 80%. So you can see the odds are stacked well against the goalkeeper. I turned this percentage around and saved 80% of penalties taken against me during my 10 years playing soccer as a junior. A goalkeeper always stands in the very centre of the goal, making it 50/50 which side the striker would place their penalty. The keeper would then have to guess one way or the other (there isn't time to watch the direction of the shot, so a guess is necessary). This would obviously make the odds of going the right way 50%, and that's not guaranteeing actually stopping the shot from going in the goal even if you guess the right way.

I had a very simple procedure. I was far more comfortable diving to my left. I would stand slightly to the right of centre in the goal. This would leave a larger space to my left, so any attacker would be crazy not to aim into the larger side. By doing this I was actually manipulating the situation, controlling where the striker would hit their shot. Now all I needed to do was dive to my left a fraction of a second before they struck the ball, giving me a good opportunity of making up the extra distance to my left and a decent chance of saving the shot. This is the method which saw me save most penalties taken against me.

I completely played to my strengths and was able to manipulate a situation with considerable odds against me succeeding, into a favourable one where the odds were actually in my favour. At the time I didn't realize why every goalkeeper wasn't doing the same but there was no way I was going to divulge my secret to anyone, not even my own team mates.

CONFIDENCE REVISITED

"Share your strengths not your weaknesses"

HARBHAJAN SINGH YOGI

Now it would be worth quickly going back to address any areas where we might suffer from a lack-of-confidence.

Near the start of this Chapter we mentioned the importance of knowing our 'triggers' which could lead to a feeling of anxiety. If there are certain situations where we get these apprehensive moments we need to break the bad cycle. Any event which makes us feel bad about ourselves is not having a positive effect on our life.

If we decide that we cannot completely avoid these triggers, which is often the case, can we deal with them differently now we know where our strengths lie? Can you change the way you present yourself in certain scenarios? Can you adopt a new approach or new attitude? Can you apply what you do best to control the situation?

I'm sure you can, we all can, and this would completely turn around this part of our life. Develop confidence by doing what we are good at. If we can, we will no longer have an aspect of our life where we do not do ourselves justice because we're a nervous wreck. Instead we will appear to be a changed person, exuding expertise and self-assurance; and all it took was a different approach – **play to your strengths**.

PARTNERS IN CRIME

"You can do what I cannot do. I can do what you cannot do. Together we can do great things."

MOTHER TERESA

This is an area which is worth mentioning but not an area in which we will dwell on. This book is about *YOU*, and how *YOU* can improve *YOURSELF* by examining *YOUR* strengths and sticking to them.

But for those who are considering setting up a company, sometimes it is as one member of a partnership. If a possible partnership does present itself there are many factors to consider.

A partnership can be a good or bad idea. They require a lot of thought and consideration. Personality types of all the individuals must be considered before a good working relationship is to be formed, and like all good relationships, these personalities need to complement each other. The skills of each person also need to be closely examined. It needs to be clear what strengths each person is bringing in to the partnership, and all people involved need to be comfortable with that. If the partnership is to be successful there can be no egos. Each must know what they are best at and what the other person/people are better at. Every member needs to feel important and valued. Each person must feel confident enough to display their strengths and secure enough not to inhibit the other partner(s) from doing what they are strongest at.

If these factors suit one another then it is possible to form a business partnership. Great things can be achieved with two or more skillsets and personalities in the equation; but be careful of the old phrase "too many cooks spoil the broth".

Richard, a close friend of mine, owns an IT company. The company manages an array of different websites and employs people in several countries across Europe. He and a friend who worked together in America for a few years set it up while they were both in their early twenties. Both were exceptional computer programmers, with Richard being particularly advanced in his technical know-how. Together they set up a business partnership and ten years on they have a very profitable business. It is obvious that they play to their strengths. Richard (who is not an especially dynamic personality) is the programming expert while his partner is the face of the company, the salesman if you will, as he has a notably outgoing personality. His role is in customer relations, to generate and maintain business connections. They are an excellent example of a successful duo with complementary skills.

TURN POSSIBILITY INTO PROBABILITY

"Success is achieved by developing our strengths, not by eliminating our weaknesses."

MARILYN VAS SAVANT

When we embark on a journey of anything new, it can be daunting, and it can involve risk. If someone decides they are in the wrong career, or maybe realizes they need a new approach, it can be extremely unnerving to change. There is a **risk/reward balance**. Is the risk worth the reward, or is the risk simply too great?

Risk is the exposure, or possible exposure to danger. Uncertainty is risk. If we are uncertain of the method or of an outcome then the risk greatly increases. Surely if we could minimize risk, or take risk out of the equation completely, then we would be left with a very appealing equation of effort = reward (we examine effort = reward in Chapter 6). Playing to our strengths completely minimizes risk.

'Playing' the stock market *can* be an incredibly uncertain 'game', even to the most seasoned investors. Experts in this field must still acknowledge that there will always be factors out of their control, such as fluctuations in global economy which can be brought about by country elections, terrorism or even something as unpredictable as natural disasters. These can ruin even the most solid investment portfolio. The possible gains can often be great which tempts people to take a higher risk on certain stocks or shares. The risk/reward balance is high. High risk but high reward. Would you be wealthy enough, brave enough or crazy enough to take on this risk?

Other areas provide a low risk/reward balance. For example, a 'safe bet'. Betting on a certain winner in a game of squash can offer very little risk, but the gains will be tiny. High investment yields low rewards, which is a risk in itself.

No bank, insurance company, stock index, or betting website will offer their customers a completely fair deal. Why would they? They are out to make money. So, in life we cannot have it both ways - small risk with big reward - or can we?

Doing what we're best at minimizes risk, without minimizing the reward. The reward of self-improvement and bettering our career remains the same, while the risk is greatly minimized. We would be in much more control of our own destiny. We'd be doing what we're best at. We would enjoy it. We would be willing to continually strive for further and further improvement, increasing our odds of success, and even increasing the possible rewards.

I hope you understand what I am saying here. If we place ourselves in a situation which we can fully control with our expertise and skills, the uncertainties are massively reduced, so therefore reducing the risk. Reduced risk equals a considerably greater possibility of success.

Turn possibility into probability.

WHAT ABOUT WEAKNESSES?

"Build upon our strengths, and your weaknesses will gradually take care of themselves."

UNKNOWN

Focus on what you can do instead of what you can't do. That's how you make yourself valuable.

Our strengths are the spring-board to our success. They not only give us the opportunity to complete tasks, achieve mastery and create a super-strength, but most importantly they give us confidence. Confidence that we can better ourselves; confidence that we can shine and distinguish ourselves from others. We excel by maximizing our strengths, never by just focusing solely on our weaknesses. However, trusting and focusing on our strengths is not the same as ignoring our weaknesses altogether.

What about our weaknesses? Yes, we cannot become an expert in any field if we have glaring weaknesses which are fundamental to achieving our goals. It would be naïve to assume our strengths could hide any obvious weaknesses to such an extent that we could still obtain the very top rewards available to us.

"It's easier to become great at something you're good at than great at something you're bad at."

ELSIE LARSON

We must accept some weaknesses are innate, and while they can be improved they can never be as strong as our strengths can be. This is why it was incredibly important when we were planning our goals and assessing our strengths that we targeted the correct career or field of expertise for the attributes we personally have. If we did plan well it is possible we will not have any obvious weaknesses in our chosen line of work. It is likely though that we will require particular skills to a level we cannot currently claim to have. Therefore improvement is probably needed in areas which we would not be particularly fond of or passionate about, so therefore drive and motivation could be an issue in order to boost our competence in certain areas. How can we combat this issue?

When we are faced with obstacles or setbacks, they will undoubtedly prompt us to question ourselves. Remember; our journey is geared to use our strengths as a focus to motivate overall growth. Self-improvement is exactly that - improving ourselves, which may also include improving weaknesses. Any weaknesses are only an issue if they are holding back our strengths. We must never prevent or restrict our strengths. It is paramount for our plan's success to utilize our strongest aspects to their maximum potential. These strengths are key to our success. Any weak areas we have only need to be developed to a level so that they can support our strengths and possibly enable our super-strength to come into play.

As our overall performance increases we will find our weaker aspects will also improve as we become more confident and skilled. As we know, confidence is a huge factor for improvement. Once we start to see promising results our confidence will increase dramatically meaning we will show less hesitation toward our weaker skills. Weaker skills will naturally step up to support our strengths.

We should only look to develop our weaknesses when we feel the time is right. This should be after we have made a solid start to our structured action plan and hit several of our mini-goals. Our confidence must be high in order to improve our weaknesses. We must not address our weaknesses when we feel down. This can only serve to dampen our spirit and our positivity toward our chance of success. So, timing is essential before addressing any weaknesses – as is how we go about improving them.

We must never spend time focusing solely on our weaknesses, always tie them into our strengths. If we can see our weaker areas improving to greater support our strengths, so therefore increasing the likelihood of using our strengths in a competitive environment, then we will start to feel incredibly positive in our abilities and with it our chances of reaching our goals. It is all about choosing the right time and knowing that we should never isolate our weaknesses for long periods; this can only lead to disillusionment.

PASS THE BATON

"Master your strengths. Outsource your weaknesses"

RYAN KAHN

Know your strengths - do those things. Know your weaknesses -

don't do those things.

Some of the world's best leaders, entrepreneurs and businessmen have a certain skill in common – they delegate. They know exactly where their strengths lie and exactly where they do not. The quote above by TV career coach Ryan Khan, says it perfectly: master your strengths, outsource your weaknesses.

Outsourcing is the new 'buzzword' for external delegation. Outsourcing is a practice used by different companies to reduce costs by transferring portions of work to outside suppliers rather than completing it internally. It is an effective cost-saving strategy when used properly. Outsourcing is the use of external help (people or companies from outside your firm), whereas to delegate is generally making use of internal support (people inside your firm).

Virgin frontman Richard Branson is recognized as being a fantastic delegator. He says: "It's vital to the success of your business that you learn to hand off those things that you aren't able to do well." Delegation is a partnership of sorts and like we covered in 'Partners in Crime', to create the perfect partnership we need to understand what strengths we bring to the boardroom and what areas we could use some help with.

To delegate/outsource is not a show of weakness, but merely a show of strength. It is the knowledge of ourselves; knowing what to personally take on and knowing what not to take on. If an expert or somebody else available to us can do a certain thing better than we can, let them. It takes vison to allow other people to add to our overall growth, and to help achieve our goal. It is a vital process for a leader such as Richard Branson in order to step back to see the master plan, and not get bogged down with the minutia of every task or job. We must accept who we are and where our strengths do and do not lie.

Let's imagine an example of a school principal who cannot delegate. In general terms a principal's overall job requirement expects them to provide a dynamic and inspirational leadership for their teaching team and pupils in order to create a positive environment where each child can thrive and fulfil their full potential. This requires an array of physical skills along with extensive planning and time management. If they do not delegate or even outsource certain tasks they could find themselves doing all kinds of extra work for example; the school financial accounts, meeting with parents, covering lessons when teachers are off, revising school policies, devising engaging new ways in which the curriculum is to be delivered, putting up wall displays, attending after-school meetings, going on courses, establishing new community links, observing teachers and examining lesson quality, disciplining naughty children, energizing underperforming teachers… and that's just on a Monday! Phew, quite a workload – and a workload which will distract them from seeing the bigger picture.

There would be no possible way any person could maintain that workload and still deliver a high performance, not to mention holding on to their sanity and health under this level of strain. Taking on extra jobs will reduce their efficiency, compromising their ability to achieve the overall goals for the school. In this situation the principal would need to pass certain jobs on to the deputy, otherwise they will be 'spread too thin' and do none of the jobs well enough. They would be too busy with no time to assess and reflect, they'd be too exhausted to offer any inspiration to anyone and quickly they would lose sight of the bigger picture and fail to deliver what is required of them – providing dynamic leadership and a positive environment in which pupils can thrive.

Overworking creates underperformance.

It is not good enough to do 10 tasks in a hectic manner delivering mediocre results, when you could be doing 3 or 4 tasks very well and delivering outstanding results. The skill of delegation is an absolutely essential one as a leader… but do not panic if you are not a natural delegator, it can be learned. The first step is to recognize the essential role of delegation, then with time and experience we can all learn how to let go just a little, and we'll soon see the bigger picture.

SO…

By now, you must have an idea of your strengths, even if you haven't yet spent time to accurately assess yourself.

Are you an Achiever or not?

If you are, do you have the belief to take a 'leap of faith', back yourself to follow your skills and instigate change? If you do, you will figure out where to begin shortly after finishing this book. I have confidence in you.

Or if you are not a strong Achiever type personality and you are happy working where you are, or if you don't want to 'rock the boat', there are still huge reasons for you to perform to the best of your ability. Doing so will give you confidence. Confidence in your specific strengths will lead to improved results. Results are always noticed. This in-turn can lead to a higher position in the company, which would likely bring you a higher salary. Sound good? Now, consider a challenge you are facing? Can you readdress it and approach it in a different manner using your strengths? I'm sure you can.

Above all, show up and speak up. It is not overly cocky or bragging to take control and manipulate a situation towards your strengths. Do not assume your boss or anyone else knows the true value you bring. You must show them. Isolate your strengths; use them and your performance will improve. This is how you will show everybody your real potential. This is how you get noticed.

Remember: Playing to your strengths reinforces confidence and performance.

These last two Chapters we have covered:

-    The tried and tested technique of setting goals so you WILL follow them through.

Develop your 4 point action plan:

Create your vision.

Make it measureable.

Set benchmarks.

How will you celebrate?

-      How to identify your strengths. Use your strengths to help you select the best career path for you. These strengths are the springboard for your career. These strengths will reduce risk and greatly increase your chance of success.

From now on at the end of each Chapter I would like you to take a 10 minute 'time-out'. Sit down on your own and have a think. Think about what you have read so far. Think how it is relevant to you. Identify your strengths and what you have to offer. Grab a pen and paper and write down your thoughts and observations. We know this is an important step. Quick - write it down before you forget it. Commit it to paper. Nobody else has to see it so there's no need to feel embarrassed. It is purely for your benefit.

"Everyone is a genius. But if you judge a fish on its ability to climb a tree, it will live its whole life believing that it is stupid."

ALBERT EINSTEIN

5 SUPER-STRENGTHS

"I think it is possible for ordinary people to choose to be extraordinary."

ELON MUSK

I love this quote by Elon Musk (creator of SpaceX and more recently one of the founders of Tesla cars). It is exactly what this Chapter is about; choosing to be extra-ordinary. But surely if it was as simple as making a choice more people would be considered extraordinary? The reason there are not more people with extraordinary attributes, or more people considered masters of their trade, is because they do not know it's as simple as making a choice. We need to know how and what to choose, and when we do then yes, it is possible.

A *super-strength* is nothing to do with being a comic book superhero. Unfortunately I cannot promise that after reading this book you will be able to shoot lasers out of your eyes, freeze people with your finger-tips or be able fly! Sorry.

However, what everybody does need to realize is that a normal person can have a super-strength, in fact I believe almost anyone can develop a super-strength. All it takes is a thirst for knowledge in a particular subject, good skill acquisition in that subject, and most importantly, the desire to excel (not just to be above average).

To some extent we will need to possess the Maximizer Talent Theme. A reminder of its definition - *one who seeks to take people and projects from great to excellent.* A Maximizer looks to transform something strong into something superb. It is the perfect personality trait to give rise to super-strengths.

So far in this book we've discussed strengths and the positive effects that focusing on what we're good at will have on our performance. These strengths can be mental or physical ie. a personality trait, a physical trait, or a physical skill. We've talked about using our strengths to pave the way for our future – how we're going to implement these strengths to improve our future.

If our strength involves a physical skill, unique experiences or in-depth knowledge of a particular subject ie. our strengths are more than just a personality trait, then we would have the opportunity to create a super-strength.

To create a super-strength we must continue to focus on our strongest physical strength in order to improve it further. Accepting ones strength as 'good enough' is not good enough! Just because it is our strongest feature doesn't mean that it is as strong as it can be. Why not make it the best it can possibly be? Strive to make it better than anyone else's, or take it in a direction no-one else has yet thought of. If we can do this, it can become our 'Specialized USP'.

'Normal' people do not think this way, but we don't want to be just normal. We do not want to settle for acceptable, we want to excel - I want you to excel and be the best you can be.

The traditional idea behind identifying strengths is to highlight non-strengths ie. weaknesses. The standard response is to then accept and ignore these strengths in order to concentrate our efforts on our weaknesses so we can put them on a par with our strengths. This is practiced every day, in every work place across the world, whether it is an office, a studio, a squash court, a gym, a football field; absolutely anywhere, and it deeply frustrates me.

"One man cannot practice many arts with success."

PLATO

JACK OF ALL TRADES BUT MASTER OF NONE

I'll refer back to the end of the last Chapter - mastering our strengths will allow us to go from the possibility of success to the probability of success.

The ultimate form of power is mastery

"Mastery is not a function of genius or talent, it is a function of time and intense focus applied to a particular field of knowledge"

ROBERT GREENE

Let me tell you a secret: the world doesn't want 'all-rounders'. We no longer want people advertising they're a 'Jack of all trades' – the world is craving experts.

We are living in a time of blogging. People want information and they want it detailed, personal and specific. People do not want anything 'general' any more. The time for average has passed.

We should be willing to fully submit ourselves to our chosen strength. Look to find any extra knowledge we can get our hands on. As we accumulate more knowledge and expertise in our chosen skills, our thirst for even more information will increase. Honing in on our strengths will keep complacency at bay as we strive for further and further progress. We will see our skills develop every day through effort – it's exciting!

Hopefully by now you have identified your strongest aspects. It's brilliant that you have strengths, but could it be possible that one of your strengths does not simply have to be just that – a strength. Could it be even greater? A super-strength?

Everyone has an area of life which they are good at and one which they may consider to be a strength, but few actually continue along a path to pursue the possibilities of where that may lead. Anybody's strength can become a super-strength with the right desire and vision. Practice and experience can get us there. Nothing more, nothing less.

Here's something interesting for you to know about:

In one study of eleven thousand U.S. scientists and engineers, the desire for mastery was found to be the single best predictor of productivity.

Learning and productivity go hand in hand. If we refer back to Chapter 4 (Conquering Confidence) and look at the traits people demonstrate when they 'play to their strengths' every day in the work environment, we see that when we strive for mastery we find ourselves 'in the zone', enjoying challenges and finishing tasks while displaying rapid learning of new skills.

Darts legend, Phil "The Power" Taylor wasn't born with a superhuman pre-disposition to be the greatest 'arrow slinger' of all time, yet he became a 16-time World Champion. The same goes for sportsmen Roger Federer (19-time tennis Grand Slam Champion) and Michael Schumacher (7-time Formula 1 Championship winner). So too for businessmen you have probably never heard of like; Do Wong Chang who worked 3 jobs simultaneously before he had enough money to set up the now billion dollar company Forever 21; Guy Laliberté who worked seriously hard perfecting his trade before starting the now world famous Cirque du Soleil; Richard Desmond who followed his interests and acquired business skills which eventually has led to him being a billionaire magazine chief; and Oprah Winfrey, who was able to turn her devastatingly hard life experiences into a way to connect with billions of people.

What I am really asking of people, of you, is that we should seriously assess what we're good at, and ask ourselves the question: *What is my best skill? Can I excel in this one skill to become better than anyone else?*

The more specialized this skill, the better… And if our strength is not yet specialized then ask: *Can I break down my main strength into smaller parts?* Are you willing to work incredibly hard to specialize one of your most impressive traits into a super-strength, or can you visualize a unique path for your strength, a niche in the market based on what you can do, what you know or what you have experienced?

Whatever this potential super-strength may be, it is essential to pursue and explore it, and now more than ever in an era where people crave expertise. We may not even think that the skill we have, or the knowledge we have, or the experiences we've lived through are especially unique, but the way we apply these to everyday life and express them for everybody to see is guaranteed to be unique; because remember, we are all unique, with a unique set of skills and a unique view of life, and a unique way of delivering them to other people. We cannot underestimate the power of our uniqueness. Who we are together with our super-strength - that is our specialized USP.

How do you decide what your super-strength should be? This is easier when you are already an expert in a particular field.

I feel this Chapter is best explained by having a look at examples to show how selecting a super-strength worked massively for others. This way we can really understand the concept and advantage of developing a super-strength.

THE WILDCARD

"The truly free individual is free only to the degree of his own self-mastery. While those who will not govern themselves are condemned to find masters to rule over them."

STEVEN PRESSFIELD

Goran Ivanišević, is an ex World No.2 tennis player and the 2001 Wimbledon Champion. He is the only player to win Wimbledon as a wildcard entrant.

If anyone has seen it or can remember it, watching Goran win the Wimbledon title was incredible. I don't think I've ever felt so emotional watching sport on TV. To see another person feel that uncontrollably happy was simply wonderful to watch. It was such a 'meant-to-be' moment for the left-handed Croat.

Ivanišević's professional career had almost exclusively centred on winning this one title. Wimbledon meant so much to him, more than any other event or any ranking. He lived to one day win Wimbledon, and he finally did it during a very low time in his professional career. Due to a shoulder injury which had haunted him for nearly three years, he had gone from being ranked the World No.2 player, down to well outside the top 100. He had been runner-up at Wimbledon three times, in 1992, 1994 and 1998. Time was rapidly running out for him to achieve his one main goal - to become Wimbledon Champion.

In 2001 his ranking was not high enough to merit being in the main draw outright but because of his past performances and popularity at the event, he had been allowed a wildcard entry into the main draw. Everyone was routing for him to win. Everybody knew how much this tournament meant to him, but deep down no one actually believed he could win it, his time had passed. When he won that last winning point of the final and uncontrollably broke down into tears, it was plain for everybody to see that he had accomplished his life goal – but why was this tournament the one thing that meant so much to him? More than the World No.1 ranking, and more than the US, Australian and French Open tournaments.

Goran Ivanišević had a true super-strength, one that shaped his focus and his career. His serve was such a weapon he became particularly specialized to grass court tennis; hence winning Wimbledon became his sole focus. The Wimbledon Championships at the All England Club in London is the oldest and most prestigious tennis event in the world, and the one grass court grand slam on the tennis calendar.

From early on in his junior tennis days it was obvious Goran had a good serve aided by his above average height. He practiced and practiced and practiced it, simplifying his service action more and more to turn his strength into a super-strength. A fast serve is especially effective on a grass court because the ball skids off the surface faster that on a concrete, carpet or clay court.

After his serve, his next most powerful strength was his volleying. The traditional grass court tactics are to 'serve and volley', whereas the other surfaces are more dependent on solid ground strokes due to the longer base-line rallies. As we can see Goran based his entire training approach around becoming a grass court specialist, and it worked to achieve his one goal – winning Wimbledon.

This is a prime example of developing a niche skill and gearing your other skills to support your one super-strength in order to achieve your goal. If at an early age, Goran Ivanišević had ever accepted his good serve as 'good enough' and instead worked equally on all aspects of his game, he would never had achieved such fame. I'm sure he would have always gone on to become a successful tennis player, but not one capable of winning the most famous tennis championships in the world.

A WOLF IN SQUASH CLOTHING

"Know your strengths and take advantage of them..."

GREG NORMAN

One of my main inspirations for writing this book is former team-mate and squash icon, **Nick Matthew**. Nick (nicknamed 'The Wolf') is a 3-time World Champion, which is a remarkable achievement in a brutal sport like squash. He was the first person I ever heard mention the phrase "super-strength".

Nick has always been a great player, from his junior days to his senior days, and I should know as a fellow, similar-aged competitor! His junior achievements are not generally acknowledged, but he was always No.1 or 2 in England through all the junior age groups. His squash back then was not pretty, nor did it show obvious World Champion potential, but he was a dogged competitor. Nick's never-say-die attitude and aggressive style of play was always going to serve him well, but it was generally thought his lack of technical skills would hold him back in the future on the senior tour at a top level. After turning 19, and out of the junior age categories, he began to develop his racket skills. Slowly, his technique began to adjust.

In squash, aggressive squash is achieved through either hard hitting or volleying (or both). Nick was a great volleyer as a youngster based around his natural athleticism and hustling instincts. His new technical alterations allowed him to volley with more skill and subtlety as he matured. Soon his forehand volley drop shot became his favourite shot. At this stage in his development, with his forehand volley drop shot up to a high standard, what most people would have done would be to move on to other areas and concentrate on strengthening any weaknesses. What Nick did was to practice this forehand volley drop shot more and more so it would never let him down. He would turn it into a weapon that he could rely on whether it was the first point of the match, or the last point of a nail-biting contest when the nerves were at their maximum. This one shot would become his "super-strength".

Soon every opponent would know to keep the ball away from Nick's forehand volley and play more onto his backhand side. Aware of this tactic, most people would go away and work solely on their backhand to match up to their forehand, but not Nick. He knew that if he worked tirelessly on his backhand only, he would lose confidence in his true strength; his forehand volley drop shot. Instead he changed the way he viewed his backhand shots. He did not try to match his forehand but made his backhand almost the polar opposite. His forehand was attacking and aggressive. His backhand became careful, measured and 'tight'. 'Tight' is a squash term for making the ball stay as close to the side wall as possible, limiting your opponents' options. Nick would squeeze his opponent on the backhand side with slow accurate shots, limiting their attacking options. They would eventually feel the need to cross-court the ball onto the forehand side to create a different pattern – then bam! This is when he would pounce on his favourite forehand volley.

Nick has become a squash great, winning 3 World Championships, 3 British Open titles (the Wimbledon of squash), he's 9-time British Champion plus a plethora of other titles. Throughout all of these events he won, every opponent he played knew what his super-strength was yet they still couldn't beat him. Even on an off day (which he most definitely had, many of them in fact. No one can be at their best all of the time) his super-strength was always reliable and could always carry him across the finish line.

If at any moment we think we are too predictably good at one aspect so we need to only work on our weaknesses, forget it. As I have said and will continue to say, the world does not want 'all-rounders', they want experts. Yes, address our weaknesses but only as a way to support our super-strength, like Nick Matthew and Goran Ivanišević did. We should never forget or move away from our true strengths.

Another great example is the Irish stout beer producer, *Guinness*. I'm assuming you've heard of Guinness, you may love it or hate it, but you've heard of it. It's not a company which immediately springs to mind like Apple, Microsoft, Coca-Cola or Nike, but it is without-a-doubt a huge company with a phenomenally successful product. A reasonably niche product which has flourished for over 200 years!

They have an amazing product and they've stuck by their product, knowing how good it is. Their recipe and attention to detail is a huge super-strength*. It's astounding the level of detail Guinness apply to the scientific process their hand-picked barley goes through to make the end product so great. As demand grew it would have been tempting for Guinness to cut corners in their specific brewing procedure to save time and money to cater for demand and to increase profits. This would have been a massive mistake only yielding short term gains but massively compromising long term income as their product would have deteriorated. Branching out would also have been an option, to steer away from their niche product in order to compete with other beer companies, but they did not. They do what they do best, have stuck by it and people love them for it. Quality is the single most important detail to Guinness, and it pays dividends. They are absolute experts in one small field, and they have never wavered from it. In fact over the centuries, they have continually looked to refine the process further and further, striving to make the same great product even better.

I have a close friend who has worked with Guinness and seen what an amazing product they have.

SPECIALIZE NOT COMPROMISE

"I don't compromise my values and I don't compromise my work."

MICHAEL MOORE

Now let's look at the flip side, if you stray away from your strengths too soon, it will have an adverse effect.

A very interesting modern day case is that of the sportswear brand **Under Armour**. Under Armour, begun in 1996 and is one of the fastest growing companies of all time, in any industry. In recent years they have almost caught up sportswear giants Nike and Adidas in terms of sales. Now, at the time of writing, Under Armour are having a tough time - for the first time in their short history their sales are down. And not just by an inconsequential amount, but by nearly 60%. Don't get me wrong, they are still doing amazingly well but this is quite a hurdle for them to overcome. I am sure it will not be a permanent problem but merely a stumbling block; but why has this situation arisen?

Some people may know that it all began with a young American man, 23 years of age at Maryland University called Kevin Plank. He was an American Football player. Using his experiences of sweat-soaked t-shirt under garments, he went on to design a tight fitting moisture wicking t-shirt to go underneath his main shirt. To cut a long story short, he gave some of his newly designed t-shirts to his Maryland friends and teammates, some of whom went on to play in the NFL. People began to take notice of his brand when a front page photo of USA Today featured Oakland Raiders quarterback Jeff George wearing an Under Armour shirt.

Under Armour was given a huge kick-start when Plank was asked to provide clothing for the 1999 hit film Any Given Sunday. Almost overnight Under Armour became a massive success. Revenue was mounting rapidly. From 2013 onwards Under Armour had not only surpassed well established brands like Puma, Reebok and Asics in US sports apparel sales, but they had also overtaken giants Adidas. At this current time of writing in early 2017, figures released later this year will show growth is down after their efforts to conquer Europe. What has let them down?

Under Armour began as a niche product. The creator was an excellent American Football player. This exposure to NFL at a high level is his strength. He used his strength; his specific experience and knowledge to design a single product that was needed for his sport. The t-shirt under layer was born. This 'base' layer t-shirt is Kevin Plank's super-strength – a specific product in a specific sport he knows very well.

Under Armour continued to produce only base layers for many years. Naturally a time would come that they would branch out to produce standard sports t-shirts catering for most sports, gym goers and running enthusiasts (and no one can blame or criticize them for this; as I said it was a natural progression). Soon footwear would follow. This was all going very well because it was still happening in another of Under Armour's strength zones; North America. They know this region well and how it functioned. This is where their origins lie. Their origins of NFL expertise, a sport almost unique to North America. Expansion proved easy in North America. Problems came when they started to spread too quickly in order to compete with Adidas in Europe. All of a sudden they started to move away from their strengths, and super-strength. They are producing regular all-sport apparel which is not their strength, and in an area of the world away from where they know best. The European market proved more difficult to conquer than expected.

Looking at these facts it is no surprise their growth has taken a hit. They have spent a lot of money trying to break into Tennis, Rugby and Soccer because they know they are the most popular sports in Europe. Expansion into Europe has not had the instant impact they hoped for or have become accustomed to in North America. As I said, I am sure Under Armour will work this out but it does show that moving away from your strength zones too quickly will usually have negative consequences.

The Body Shop: The Body Shop is a British cosmetics and skin care shop, with stores worldwide.

The company was founded in 1976 and was famous for being extremely anti animal testing. They always made a big show of this which endeared people to the brand. This was their USP in a rapidly growing cosmetics market with more and more brands to compete with. They were doing great.

In 2006 the company was sold to French cosmetic giants L'Oreal, for close to $1 Billion. Shortly after, claims that L'Oreal used animal testing created media controversy as it was totally against The Body Shop's core values. Over the next 10 years the brand's popularity and revenue decreased. This year L'Oreal have sold The Body Shop for a substantial loss.

Two good examples that compromising your brand and not staying true to your strengths will have a negative impact. People like experts and they love an individual or unique story. Once something becomes 'general' or 'generic' people lose interest.

SO…

Recap:

-    You know how to set a 4 point action plan to reach your goal.

Write your goals down. In fact, if you're happy doing so, write as much down as you like along your journey to creating an improved, more productive you. Write down every success, every time you have celebrated, and every time you've hit a stumbling block.

-    Take time to know your strengths, if you don't already know them. These strengths will guide you to identify what you should be doing in your career.

Use the personality test. Examine Whipp's Tiered Talents. Are you an Achiever?

Know your skill set.

-    Do you want to develop mastery? Can you see the benefit of creating a specialist skill? Do you have a skill you can further hone to develop your very own super-strength?

Specialize, not compromise.

How are you going to use the information you've read so far? How will you apply it to develop a new strategy to stand out from the crowd? Develop a modus operandi (MO) using your strengths. An MO you believe in. One which brings the best out in you and gives you confidence. Your unique MO which you can trust will not let you down.

Don't be afraid to specialize.

Do not shy away from your strengths or leave them unattended. A strength which is simply 'good enough' is not good enough to stand out from the crowd. Do not compromise on what you do best for short term gains. You have the opportunity to turn your most prominent strength into a super-strength.

Take your strongest strength and seek ways to make it even stronger. Research it, practice it, look to perfect it, until you can consider yourself a master. Strive to be better than anyone else, no matter how small or specialized this one skill may be. You will love the process of doing so, but know this - there is no shortcut. It does not happen overnight, but every hour of effort you put in is an hour well spent. Slowly and surely you will be moving along the path toward mastery.

This is your opportunity to create a Specialized USP for yourself. This will be what you become respected for among your peers. This is what you can charge extra money for, or what will earn you real distinction in your career.

Time to reflect for 10 minutes before turning the page. Think about everything you've read and how you will use this information to your advantage.

"Mastery is not a question of genetics or luck, but of following your natural inclinations and the deep desires that stirs you from within."

ROBERT GREENE

6 THE COMMITMENT COMMODITY

"There's a difference between interest and commitment. When you're interested in doing something, you do it only when it's convenient. When you're committed to something, you accept no excuses; only results."

KENNETH BLANCHARD

Do not be found guilty of committing the ultimate crime of self-improvement – the crime of non-committal.

How will anybody achieve anything great if they do not fully commit to it? They won't is the answer.

When working with top athletes on a daily basis this is clearly evident. Players who hold back or look for excuses, will not reach the very top, and they will not achieve their goals (unless their goals are pathetic in the first place which is signaling to everybody that they are setting themselves up for failure or they just want an easy life). Players who set difficult goals, who fully commit whatever the circumstances or whatever setbacks may happen along the way, and who apply drive and discipline to everything they do in pursuit of their goal; they are the ones who stand a very good chance of realizing their dreams. This is exactly the same in business.

I know my experiences so far are largely sport based, but the parallels between sport and business are huge. In both sport and business, success doesn't just happen; it comes from drive, desire, motivation, discipline, adaptation and the willingness to learn and improve. Under-achievers will refer to these traits as 'obsession', but we know that these are not negative traits. They are incredibly positive traits which can lead to great success. People who are driven in this way have a thirst for success and feel much satisfaction from accomplishing their targets.

Richard Branson, founder of Virgin and one of the world's most successful entrepreneurs, recently went on record to say he would actively look to hire ex-professional sportsmen because of their positive attitude toward hard work and their first-hand experience of what it takes to succeed. Nobody pushes themselves to the absolute limit like a world-class athlete. They know that in order to be the best this is the minimum requirement of what must be done.

NEW YEAR, NEW EXCUSES

"Always bear in mind that your own resolution to succeed is more important than any other."

ABRAHAM LINCOLN

In the first week of January every year, millions of people make New Year Resolutions. This is soon followed by millions of people giving up on their resolutions, which usually happens by the middle of January! Research at Scranton University showed just 8% of people who make a New Year Resolution actually go on to achieve their goal. People have become far too accustomed to failure.

Most people who make resolutions don't have any idea about goal setting methods like we discussed in Chapter 3. Almost none of these 'resolution setters' will actually write their resolution down or have any idea how to make a realistic 'action plan' involving mini goals or stepping stones on their journey to realizing their overall goal.

The most common New Year Resolutions are: Exercise more (38%), lose weight (33%), and to eat more healthily (32%). As we can see, by far the most common desires people have at this time of year are health related, specifically weight orientated. To change habits, and to change ones health or physical appearance isn't easy. This requires effort, commitment and follow-through. It involves resisting what is easy and comfortable. Weak people will always gravitate toward what is easy and comfortable. Who doesn't want to be comfortable? **It is easier to fail than to do what is demanded to succeed.**

MONKEY BUSINESS

~

THE CHIMP BRAIN

"You have to keep your chimp in the cage - your chimp is your emotional side, and in a pressure situation you have to react with logic not emotion"

BRADLEY WIGGINS

So this brings me nicely on to the Chimp Brain. You may or may not have heard of this before. It is that area of your brain which allows failure. It allows for excuses.

Weak people are controlled by their Chimp Brain. Strong people are not.

We all know our brain has different sections, each offering different functions. Here's a bit of basic science: It is in the outer edge of the brain, known as the cortex, where thinking takes place. This is our 'grey matter'. If the outer edge had just one area for thinking we wouldn't have a problem. However, there are at least two thinking and interpreting areas. The dorso-lateral edge is interpreting input in a rational and logical way.

The orbito-frontal cortex interprets by impression, feelings and emotions, and has direct links to the amygdala. The amygdala is a fast acting defence mechanism that does not think but responds, and responds quickly. So, this second way of thinking has 'joined forces' with the strongest emotional centre within the brain, the amygdala.

What we have in effect are two interpreting brains. One of them (the orbito-frontal cortex) is virtually automatic and thinks for us without our input and is based on emotion. The other (dorso-lateral edge) is under our control and allows us to think rationally, as we want to. The trouble is that these two 'brains' do not think the same way and they do not typically agree on the interpretation of what is going on. We have a potential "battle" going on all the time within our head!

"How can you determine who you really are? To work out who you really are as a person is easy to do. If you wrote a list of all the things you would like to be, you may write things like calm, compassionate, reasonable, positive, confident and happy, then this is who you really are. Any deviation from this is a hijacking by the Chimp."

STEVE PETERS

The Chimp Model offers a simplified way of understanding our two thinking brains and how we can learn to use them to the best of our ability. The model is neither pure scientific fact nor a hypothesis. It is a simple representation to aid understanding and help us to use the science. It may also help us to make sense of how we have been in the past, how we are now, and how we can manage ourselves better in the future.

The Inner Chimp is the emotional team within the brain that thinks and acts for us without our permission. The Logical Brain is the real person, it is you at your best; rational, compassionate and humane, and is the Human within… but is generally harder to engage.

'Chimp Comments' are all too popular and can be heard every single day; in every office, every gym, every classroom and in every home. Here's some examples:

It's too cold to eat healthy food.

If I cycle to the gym, then I'll be too tired for my workout.

I would eat broccoli but I don't like it.

I'm too busy to exercise.

I don't have the time to…

I can't afford the gym.

It's raining.

I don't have the will power to quit smoking.

I'm too tired.

I'm too self-conscious to exercise.

I tried but I wasn't very good.

The treadmill is boring.

Now, take 2 minutes and think of some Chimp Comments. It's actually good fun. All you have to do is make up a ridiculous excuse and somebody somewhere will probably be saying it right now.

When we do this simple exercise we quickly realize how pathetic these comments sound. I also find myself immediately thinking of the counter argument. Hopefully you too will find that your Logical Brain kicks in to counteract your Inner Chimp.

Now, re-read the above Chimp Comments and imagine it's your close friend saying them to you. What should you say in reply to keep them on track and to prevent them from giving up on their goal, whatever that may be. What is your counter argument for each remark?

My counter arguments would be:

It's too cold to eat healthy food – *healthy food is not just a cold salad. It can be a hot or cold meal. You can have a heart-warming soup or a freshly prepared warm meal which is full of healthy vitamins and minerals.*

If I cycle to the gym, then I'll be too tired for my workout – *the body is capable of phenomenal things, and a 20 minute cycle won't come close to effecting your potential to perform, in fact it will serve as an excellent warm up and enable you to perform even better when you reach the gym. Just think of the extra calories you could*

85

burn.

I would eat broccoli but I don't like it – *choose an alternative vegetable. There's literally dozens of alternative options, and you must like some of them.*

I'm too busy to exercise – *make time. It's a question of priorities. Adding value to certain tasks (like exercise for example) and making time for what's important. If you're stressed because you're "too busy" then exercise can only help. Everyone knows about the positive effect exercise has on the human brain. Endorphins can de-stress a person, lead to a feeling of happiness and relaxation.*

I don't have the time to... – *exercise doesn't have to take hours out of your day. It can be 50 sit ups before you go to bed, press ups at home, a 20 minute jog around your local roads, a small circuit of exercises off YouTube or buy a cheap exercise bike to have at home then you don't waste time travelling to the gym. If it's eating healthy or cooking which you don't have time for, then start by replacing sweet treats with fruit, and no extra time has been wasted. Order shopping online instead of having to drive to the supermarket. You save time and will buy less "bad products" which were purchased because you picked it off the shelf on a whim, or you were hungry and you wanted a snack for the drive home, or the packaging looked nice etc.*

I can't afford the gym – *exercise at home or go for a run. Most people these days have access to two or more gyms within 5 miles of their home or workplace, and all at different price ranges. Choose the cheapest. Budget and prioritize exercise – eg. if you didn't spend as much money on alcohol at the weekend, you could use what you save to pay for your gym membership.*

I don't have the will power to quit smoking – *You absolute CHIMP! Everyone has the will power, it's the desire, commitment and follow-through you lack. No sacrifice feels easy at first, but it will get easier. It will feel so good, and quicker than you think.*

"All things are difficult before they are easy."

THOMAS FULLER

I'm too tired – *exercise actually energizes you, you just have to force yourself to do it initially. Start off lightly and increase it only when you feel ready, but importantly make a start. You will soon get in a routine of exercising.*

I'm too self-conscious to exercise – *you don't have to wear the sexiest Lycra available, or have the best running technique. Realize everyone feels self-conscious about something, but don't let your insecurities stop you. The only way to feel better about your insecurities is to do something about it. Face your fears.*

I tried but I wasn't very good – *no body is a master or World Champion at anything the first time. It's not about being the best immediately, it's about doing it and enjoying the small improvement each week. EVERY EXPERT WAS ONCE A BEGINNER.*

The treadmill is boring – *then use the bike, the rowing machine, the stepper or another piece of gym equipment. Maybe go for a run outside. Vary your routine. Don't do long aerobic stints, maybe do circuits of different exercises, or Zumba, or spinning. There are many options out there to make exercising more enjoyable.*

Exercise and healthy eating become almost addictive because of the great feeling they give us: We feel more energetic, we sleep better, we'll be less stressed, we will have a desire to smile, we even work harder, and we will look great too. Our confidence improves greatly and we feel like we can do anything and take on any challenge.

Whether it's eating differently, exercising, studying or beginning a new task – we must make a start. Push though the hard beginning. Put any Chimp Comments to one side and let our Logical Brain lead us. We'll quickly develop a routine, and even more powerfully than that, we'll genuinely want to continue.

When we are about to start something new, or difficult, or daunting, we must harness our Logical Brain and allow ourselves to listen to it whenever we are on the verge of making a Chimp Comment. No excuses. With practice the Logical Brain will become the first stop for our thoughts, meaning we can over-ride our Chimp Brain immediately after sensory input. Remember; the Logical Brain is our voice of reason.

So we can see, whether we already are or want to be an Olympian, an international footballer, an entrepreneur, a high performing teacher or a successful business leader, we need to tame our Inner Chimp. We must let our Logical Brain control our decision making. This Logical Brian will control our path to success, whereas our Chimp Brain will hold us back and lead us down a path toward failure.

WHAT A FEELING, WHEN WE'RE DANCING ON THE CEILING

"Learning to celebrate success is a key component of learning how to win in the market."

DOUGLAS CONANT

However we do not want to completely detach from our chimp brain, we need to keep our Chimp Brain active but on our terms - when we choose to let it out. It is here when we can allow ourselves to feel the full emotion of every 'stepping stone' reached, and every minor victory on our way toward our end goal. We know rewarding ourselves is a necessary step of goal achievement, just be careful we do not let the 'monkey out the cage' when we experience an obstacle or setback; this is the exact situation where we must use our Logical Brain to remain rational and calm. Decisions in the 'heat of the moment' when we let our Chimp Brain govern our reaction can completely break us and ruin everything we've worked so hard for.

Respond not react.

(We will look more closely at dealing with a setback in Chapter 8)

SO...

Do not allow your Chimp Brain to affect your commitment. You must follow-through on your goals, otherwise you're no different from the 92% of people who simply quit. Nobody wants to be a quitter, especially when you know you have more to give. Commitment and follow-through on your goals will lead to massive self-improvement, and even wealth.

Here's what we've covered so far:

-    Think what you want to achieve and write your goal down, then break it down into smaller, more easily achievable mini-goals.

-    We all have personality and physical strengths. What is your personality type and how will you use your strongest traits to address that work problem tomorrow?

What skills do you have? How will you use these every day.

-    Which of your skills can you focus more attention on? Do you feel you have one skill which when mastered, will separate you from everybody else around you?

-    You must show complete commitment to your goals, otherwise you will not succeed.

Don't be shy. Self-Improvement and progress is completely in your hands.

"There is but one degree of commitment; TOTAL"

ARNIE SHERR

7 EFFORT = REWARD

"My father says that if I hit 2500 balls each day, I'll hit 17,500 balls each week, and at the end of one year I'll have hit nearly one million balls. He believes in math. Numbers, he says, don't lie. A child who hits one million balls each year will be unbeatable."

ANDRE AGASSI

People aren't born geniuses, they get there through effort.

In today's society people are looking for a shortcut or fast track course to success. With the birth of the internet and now social media, several cases have come to light where people have hit upon something great which has had almost instant popularity and recognition, and they've become what seems like over-night millionaires. Social media has shared these stories so everybody knows about them. It is dangerous for our society to know of these cases because it makes people believe there is a shortcut for everyone, so people become lazy and often bitter. They think one of two ways: that these few have been so lucky and it could never happen to them; or that there is an easy way for everyone to get rich, they just need to hit upon the right idea or opportunity. This makes them impulsive and fickle, moving from idea to idea with no stamina and very little effort. These people quit very quickly to move on to the next 'get rich quick' scheme.

In reality, the successful cases have been considerably glamorized. The media want to document stories about big sales and money making. Nobody's interested in hearing long stories about the mundane day to day grafting, failed attempts and years of effort, instead they jump straight to the end which gives people an incredibly false sense of effort = reward.

For example, let's have a quick look at Ray Dalio. For those of you who don't know who he is, he's one of the world's greatest investors and the most successful hedge fund manager in history - known as 'the Steve Jobs of Investing'. Dalio is the founder of Bridgewater Associates, the largest hedge fund in the world, managing almost $170 billion!

Dalio was born into a family with no investment background. He began investing at the age of 12 while he was working as a golf caddy. 'Wall Streeters' used to frequent his golf course and he began to learn from their conversations. After a lucky start, a few more stock purchases followed and very quickly he was (as he says) "hooked" on playing the stock market.

By the time Ray went to college he had already built a portfolio worth several thousand dollars. He went on to University and business school where he also worked on the floor in the New York Stock Exchange. He later worked as the Director of Commodities at an investment and merchant banking company before moving on to another Wall Street firm. In 1975, at the age of 26, Ray Dalio founded Bridgewater Associates out of his apartment.

When you hear that someone started a company at the age of 26 and has gone on to become one of the richest men in America, it sounds pretty cushty right? Actually it took years of research and experience in his particular field before he was competent enough to start up his own company. The fact he began his experiences at such a young age obviously helped him. During his years of advanced studies and working for several companies, he excelled at his job and built up a loyal client base. Taking many of these favoured investors with him, this is what enabled him to start his company so successfully when he was still in his mid-twenties.

At the age of 26, Ray Dalio had most definitely gained more experience through more hours of concentrated effort than his peers of a similar age. This is what enabled him to stand out from the crowd and succeed. This success did not come easily. And let's not forget, this is only what got him to the stage of getting started in business. Success was not guaranteed, far from it. For him to turn Bridgewater Associates into a massive success took an incredible amount of effort along the way. It was not an 'overnight success'. There were many mistakes and many opportunities to learn from these mistakes in a sector of business whose very nature can be unpredictable and volatile.

Investing in stocks and shares at the age of 12 is not a pre-requisite to succeed in the stock market; just as one would not have to become a computer programmer as a child in order to work in the computer software business later in life, or learn to design clothes at junior school in order to own a chain of high street stores. Sure it helps, and can speed things up when we are in our twenties, but is not a necessary condition of success. There are many cases of people who have succeeded much later in life which we will have a look at later in this Chapter.

TALENT IS A MYTH

"The most difficult thing is the decision to act, the rest is merely tenacity."

AMELIA EARHART

Stanford University psychologist Carol Dweck proposes there are two mindsets we can live by: A **Fixed Mindset** - where a person believes intelligence, talent and ultimately success are traits we are born with; we either have them or we don't; or a **Growth Mindset** – where we believe we can improve. If we have a growth mindset we see ourselves as a lifelong learner.

Effort = Reward - You may think that this is an obvious concept but actually it seems not to be. You would be amazed how many of the population think that the high achievers in life are either lucky, were in the right place at the right time, have success handed to them on a silver platter, or have 'God-given' talent that they're incredibly blessed to have, so they themselves don't stand a chance of competing with these lucky few! Most people believe that these select few, and only these few, were somehow hand pinked by divine intervention to be the ones to carry our human population forward with their achievements.

It's easier for people to think that this tiny percentage of the human race are completely set apart from the rest of the world, and they are somehow not real people but super-humans. They are the X-Men of the real world, the 0.000000001% of the population that are born with a genetic mutation to make them succeed. It's so much simpler for the average person's brain to accept that these rich or successful people were born to be great, so what's the point in even trying to match them or achieve great successes of their own. So many people think that if they try they will obviously fail because they are not lucky enough to have had this divine intervention which turned them into a superhuman, so it's best not to try when success is given, not earned. The people who think this way are completely governed by their Chimp Brian.

The fact you are reading this book, I'm going to assume you are not the average person with a defeatist, fixed attitude, and you are looking for ways in which you can improve yourself and become part of the successful elite. You have a growth mindset. You believe it is possible to be someone who really achieves in life; whether this is as one of the top performers in your office or as a 'solo-artist' of some kind. I hope you read the paragraphs above and are either incredibly shocked or even pity the people who think like that. The fact is they make up most of the worlds' population. How depressing is that? I also hope you are the type of person who is willing to put in the effort required and you are the type of person who can be inspired by others' achievements instead of threatened by them.

"If you work hard and meet your responsibilities, you can get ahead, no matter where you come from, what you look like or who you love."

BARACK OBAMA

For years and years these daft people who are controlled by their Chimp Brain have bewildered me. Why can they not see that putting in more effort will achieve more, no matter who they are? If we take tennis for example; it is a sport which most people like to watch, and most people can appreciate. Whether they are an avid fan, or just show a casual interest from time to time, they are able to offer an opinion.

They can offer an opinion on who they like to watch and who they would like to win. When we see two people competing against each other we have a deep-set human instinct to favour one competitor over the other and decide who we would like to win.

Now let's specifically look at Roger Federer, the greatest tennis player of all time. The one comment we hear countless times about Federer is "He's great because he's so talented". It's said by our neighbour who has no idea about the complexities of the sport, our mate who plays a bit of tennis at his local club, and even by so-called experts in the commentary box and in the media. Dismissing Federer's achievements as pure talent is a complete dis-service to the awesome man. It's a complete Chimp comment. What people are actually telling themselves is 'he's lucky because he has an unexplainable natural gift for tennis and that is what makes him so great. It would not be fair to compare a 'normal' person to him!' These people think it's been easier for him to succeed because of his 'natural talent' and that's why they themselves could never replicate what he has done. It is their justification to themselves to forgive the fact that they never try. That way they never have to experience the sacrifices, the commitment or pain and suffering that he has been willing to put himself and his family through.

What it has actually taken for Roger Federer to achieve what he's achieved is hours and hours... and hours of hard work; perfecting his technique, his movement, his strategy, and his focus. It's taken a gargantuan commitment. He's been willing to sacrifice most things a normal young man takes for granted; weekends with mates drinking, eating unhealthy treats whenever he likes, staying up late to binge on episodes of Game Of Thrones, going for an afternoon game of golf with friends, and countless other simple pleasures we all regularly enjoy. It takes a man who can control his Chimp Brain so he can visualize all the possibilities his dedication could lead to. It takes a desire to be the best, but not only that; but to also be willing to do everything in his power to make it happen, no matter what the cost.

It's natural to look at Roger Federer and compare him to Rafael Nadal, his fiercest rival. They have both been No.1 and 2 in the world for almost a decade, playing every major final against one another, and both collecting every significant tennis trophy numerous times. Due to his appearance and style of play, Nadal looks more committed. His muscles are bigger, his style of play is more attritional and he smiles less. All these attributes give the uneducated viewer a perceived sense that he has trained harder than Roger to make up for his unequal amount of 'God-given talent'. People assume he has spent more hours in the gym, more time crafting strategies of play to wear his opponent down, and he's probably employed sports psychologists to help him remain focused during his brutal 5 hour matches.

The fact is, Rafael Nadal has not spent more dedicated hours to his tennis than Roger Federer has. Rafael Nadal does not have less 'talent' than Roger Federer. The two players have different strengths so therefore have dedicated their time to different aspects of their tennis; but importantly we need to know that they will have spent the same amount of time dedicated to their tennis to make them as good as they can be.

Roger Federer will have spent more hours than we can imagine grooving his forehand technique, combining this technique with patters of movement that make him fast and balanced on every shot. This makes his forehand drives look effortless, but to reach this point his forehand drives have been far from effortless. His forehand shots are a direct result of very specific actions he has chosen to take. The same goes for his backhand technique, his volley and his serve. Roger's game is based around technical combinations of shots and movements in order to expose targeted areas for the final winning strike.

Because Federer smiles more, does that make him less focused? Of course not. It is his most effective way to stay flowing and relaxed on court. Like Nadal, Federer will have worked with sport psychologists and will have spent hours of his day, every day, thinking about physical and mental strategies in order to win matches. The technique and movement work Federer has done over the years makes his game technically attractive, making him extremely appealing to watch for the tennis purists and also the unschooled spectators.

On the other hand, Rafael Nadal has chosen to spend the majority of his hours to work more on power, to turn himself into a relentless machine. His technique and his movement is different to Roger's, but is completely suitable for his style of play. His game is geared around strength and repetitiveness. Rafael's style is appealing to gym goers and people who value hard work (although we know that hard work is a perceived myth when we are to compare two top athletes in the same sport).

I very much like both these players. I admire the phenomenal hard work they have dedicated to their chosen profession in order to become the best. Neither of them ever wanted to be 'good' or 'one of the best', they both used their strengths and their immense efforts to become the 'very best'.

Hopefully now you can understand my annoyance when people refer to Roger Federer as simply "talented". I'm sure you can see this is extremely naïve and an injustice to him and the commitment he has shown behind closed doors.

Talent is a myth.

A SUPER STREET?

"It's inevitable your environment will influence what you do."

DUNCAN SHEIK

'Talent' is an interesting word, and it would be foolish of me to dismiss it totally. It's people's perception of talent as opposed to hard work which is wrong.

I do believe people can have a natural aptitude for certain physical activities. Some people most definitely have bodies more geared up to sport than others, and this is obvious from an early age. What cannot be true though is that these people have bodies designed to be great at one sport, and one sport only. Serena Williams and her sister Venus were not born to be champion tennis players. Usain Bolt was not born to be the fastest man on earth, just as Kobe Bryant was not destined just to be a basketball player.

The examples above most definitely would have stood out as good athletes when they were young. They will have shown a natural talent for sport. As mentioned in Chapter 4 concerning Rafael Nadal, it will have been their environment which ultimately dictated their sport of choice.

Rafael Nadal had two extremely sporty uncles, one being a retired professional soccer player, and the other an ex-professional tennis player. Naturally athletic Nadal quickly became very good at both sports. He carried on playing both soccer and tennis intently until the age of 12 when he made the choice to concentrate on just one sport.

Usain Bolt was also good at several sports, playing a lot of cricket and soccer at an early age. His cricket coach suggested he also try some track and field events which were popular at his high school. Quickly Usain began to focus on sprinting.

Kobe Bryant's father was an NBA player, as too was his uncle… need I say any more? I think you get the message.

Let's read this excerpt taken from Matthew Syed's book, Bounce:

> *In January 1995 I became the British No 1 table tennis player for the first time — which, I am sure you will agree, is a heck of an achievement. Table tennis is a pretty big sport in the UK, with 2.4 million participants, 30,000 paid-up members of the governing body, thousands of teams and serious riches for those who excel.*
>
> *But what made me special? What had marked me out for greatness? I came up with various attributes: speed, guile, gutsiness, mental strength, adaptability, agility and reflexes. Sometimes I would marvel that I had these skills in such abundance that they were capable of elevating me — little me! — beyond hundreds of thousands of others aspiring to that precious top spot. And all this was doubly amazing, considering that I had been born into a family in an ordinary suburb of an ordinary town in southeast England. There was no silver spoon. No nepotism. Mine was a triumph of individuality, a personal odyssey of success, a triumph against the odds.*

This, of course, is the way that many who have reached the top in sport, or indeed in any other field, choose to tell their stories. We live in a culture that encourages this kind of soaring individualism. But while these stories are inspirational, rousing and entertaining, are they true? Here is my table tennis story, retold with the bits that I chose to ignore the first time around, as they diminished the romance and individuality of my triumph.

1. **Table** *In 1978 my parents, for reasons they are still unable to explain, decided to buy a table tennis table — a super deluxe 1000 with gold lettering, since you ask — and to put it in our large garage. You can imagine that there were not many youngsters of my age (I was 8 at the time) in my home town who possessed a full-size, tournament-specification table. Fewer still had a garage in which it could be housed full-time. This was my first bit of good fortune.*

2. **My Brother** *My second piece of good fortune was having an older brother, Andrew, who came to love table tennis as much as I did. We would play for hours after school: duelling, battling, testing each other's reflexes, experimenting with new spins, investigating new paddles, inviting over friends who, although often more accomplished in other sports, were bemused to see just how far we had advanced in table tennis.*

3. **Peter Charters** *Mr Charters was a teacher at the local primary school, a tall man with a moustache, a twinkle in his eye and a disdain for conventional teaching methods. He was the coach of almost all the after-school sporting clubs, the organiser of school sports day and inventor of a game called "bucket ball", a kind of improvised basketball.*

But Charters cared about one thing above all: table tennis. He was the nation's top coach and a senior figure in the English Table Tennis Association. No child who passed through Aldryngton School in Reading was not given a try-out by Charters — and such were his zeal, energy and dedication to table tennis that anybody who showed potential was persuaded to take his or her skills forward at the local club, Omega. He invited me and my brother to join Omega in 1980, just when we were beginning to outgrow the garage.

4. **Omega** *Omega was not a luxurious club: it was a one-table hut in a gravel enclosure in suburban Reading: cold in winter, ferociously hot in summer, with plants growing through the roof and floor. But it had one advantage that made it almost unique in the county: it was open 24 hours a day for the exclusive use of its tiny group of members, each of whom had a set of keys.*

My brother and I took full advantage, training after school, before school, at weekends and during school holidays. We were joined by other Aldryngton alumni who had been spotted and snapped up by Charters, so that by 1981 Omega was becoming something of a sensation. One street alone (Silverdale Road, where the school was) contained an astonishing number of the nation's top players.

At No 119 were the Syeds. Andrew, my brother, went on to become one of the most successful junior players in the history of British table tennis, winning three national titles before retiring due to injury in 1986. Matthew (that's me) also lived at 119 and became a long-serving England senior No 1, a three-time Commonwealth champion and a two-time Olympian.

At No 274, just opposite Aldryngton, lived Karen Witt. She went on to win the Commonwealth championships and was widely considered one of the most brilliant female players of her generation. At No 149, equidistant between the Syeds and the Witts, lived Andy Wellman. He was a top national player who won a string of titles, particularly in doubles.

Down at the bottom of Silverdale Road were Paul Trott, a leading junior, and Keith Hodder, an outstanding county player. Around the corner were Jimmy Stokes (England junior champion), Paul Savins (junior international), Alison Gordon (four times English senior champion), Paul Andrews (top national player) and Sue Collier (England schools champion). I could go on.

For a period in the 1980s, this street and its immediate vicinity produced more outstanding table tennis players than the rest of the nation. One road among tens of thousands of roads; one tiny cohort of schoolkids against millions up and down the country. Silverdale Road was the wellspring of English table tennis: a ping-pong mecca that seemed to defy explanation or belief.

Had some genetic mutation spread through the area without touching the surrounding roads and villages? Of course not: the success of Silverdale Road was about the coming together of factors of a kind beguilingly similar to those that have, from time to time, elevated other tiny places into the sporting ascendancy (for example, Spartak, an impoverished Moscow tennis club, created more Top 20 women players between 2005 and 2007 than the whole of the US).

In our case, all the local sporting talent was focused ruthlessly on table tennis, and all the aspiring players were nurtured by an outstanding coach. As for me, with a table in the garage and a brother as passionate about the game as I was,

I had a head start before I even went to Aldryngton.

The message is pretty obvious – specific circumstances and hours of practice created a single street in England producing more world class table tennis players than the rest of the world combined.

Would Rafael Nadal have ended up being a professional tennis player if he lived on this street? Incredibly doubtful. How about Kobe Bryant or the Williams sisters? Would they have become an NBA or tennis legend had they lived on Silverdale Road? Of course not.

It would therefore be tempting to think that thousands of potential champions all over the world have slipped through the net, missed out on potential sporting greatness depending on where they grew up. What if a potential major-winning golfer had never been given a golf club, or a future Wimbledon champion lived 100 miles from the nearest tennis court?

I'm sure thousands of people, had they lived on Silverdale Road in the 70's and 80's, could have become a table tennis expert. What if Kobe Bryant attended Usain Bolt's school in Jamaica? How about if Usain Bolt was born into Kobe Bryant's family? I think their chosen careers would have been different, but it seems certain they would have excelled due to their natural 'talent'/aptitude for sport in general, and of course their excellent commitment and attitude toward hard work.

Ray Dalio, the billionaire hedge fund manager, was eventually shaped by his environment. Even though he was not born into a family of investors or hedge fund managers, from the age of 12 when he was exposed to "Wall Streeters" on that now life-changing golf course, he made investing his world in his spare time. He sought it out in order to immerse himself fully. This gave him the same environmental opportunities and advantages which were available to Rafael Nadal, Serena Williams, Matthew Syed etc.

Andy Murray moved to Spain when he was 15. He and his family felt a different environment was required to further his tennis career. Would Andy Murray have go on to become World No.1 if he had stayed in Scotland all of his life, where elite level competition was scarce?

Circumstance doesn't just have to be based on luck. One can seek it. And this is important to understand - otherwise you will become ruled by your Chimp Brain with feelings of jealousy, ill fortune and injustice.

Are most successful people then a beneficiary of their specific circumstances; namely their environment and their opportunities? Yes, they definitely are. Without a doubt they have benefitted, but that is nowhere near the 'be all and end all'. Without the correct personality type nothing would have been achieved. There is absolutely no substitute for relentless hard work, unwavering dedication and sacrifice.

THERE'S NO SUCH THING AS SPEEDY BOARDING

"Repetition is the mother of skill."

TONY ROBBINS

THE 10,000 HOUR RULE

There is no shortcut to greatness.

In 1990, after losing to a classmate at chess for the first time after always beating him, Anders Ericsson wanted to look into what makes somebody improve. He went on to conduct extensive research into what it takes to become an expert at a particular task. He came up with a magic number; 10,000 hours. Ericsson concluded that somebody had to practice for at least 20 hours a week, 50 weeks a year and for 10 years to achieve excellence. Not just any practice would suffice, only 'deliberate practice'.

This '10,000-Hour Rule' was really brought to the public's attention in 2008 by Malcolm Gladwell's book, 'Outliers'. Gladwell basically repeated what Ericsson had claimed 18 years earlier, although he did not stress the importance of the type of practice. Gladwell also believes that circumstance, 'luck' and genes play a major role in success.

DELIBERATE PRACTICE

"I fear not the man who has practiced 10,000 kicks once, but I fear the man who has practiced one kick 10,000 times."

BRUCE LEE

I believe it should go without saying that the importance of the type of practice that is taking place in order to achieve maximum benefit from the hours put in plays a massive role. The practice must be quality. It must be 'deliberate'. If we look at a skill which millions of people do every day – driving. Surely many of us have spent more than 10,000 hours driving, yet we're not improving. We're not doing handbrake turns into car parking spaces or if we had the opportunity we wouldn't have the ability to take a sharp hairpin bend at 150mph. This is because we are not striving for improvement. 'Deliberate practice' is not taking place. For practically everybody, driving is an almost thoughtless action performed to serve a basic function - to get us from A to B. We do not care if we are the best driver in the world, we don't need to be; here is a situation where it is good enough to be good enough. These are not conditions in which excellence or any improvement can occur.

'Deliberate practice' requires a plan and of course, attention to detail. There must be feedback and analysis of results. It is focused, it is purposeful. It is all aimed at one thing - to improve. Once we see improvement we do not stop there, we continue in order to improve even further. It's a commitment. It's dedicated. It's goal orientated... and what it is most definitely not is mindless, or simply a process of 'going through the motions'.

Geoffrey Colvin, author of 'Talent Is Overrated: What Really Separates World-Class Performers from Everybody Else', gives us a nice example of the difference between practice and deliberate practice: *Simply hitting a bucket of balls is not deliberate practice, which is why most golfers don't get better.*

Hitting an eight-iron 300 times with a goal of leaving the ball within 20 feet of the pin 80 percent of the time, continually observing results and making appropriate adjustments, and doing that for hours every day—that's deliberate practice.

AS FIT AS A FIDDLE

Ericsson's Violinists

Ericsson's study was with violinists. He took three groups of expert violinists who differed in levels of attained musical performance, but all experts nonetheless. He studied how these musicians spent their daily lives by interviewing them and having them keep detailed dairies for a week. Despite the fact that these expert violinists all spent about the same combined time practicing in all types of music-led activities, the two best groups were found to spend more time in solitary practice. When the experts practiced by themselves, they focused with full concentration on improving specific aspects of their music performance as identified by their master teachers; therefore meeting the criteria for deliberate practice. The best group of young expert violinists spent around four hours every day, including weekends, in this type of solitary practice.

From retrospective calculations this is where Ericsson calculated the figure of 10,000 hours and put it to the test on existing experts. By examining other experts in various fields of expertise he was able to support his 10,000 Hour Theory. It is generally accepted as a sound estimate.

"Excellence demands effort and planned deliberate practice of increasing difficulty."

ANDERS ERICSSON

I have examined different cases to apply his theory:

A HARD DAY'S NIGHT

The Beatles

Continuing with the musical theme; The Beatles started out their career by forcing upon themselves a brutal schedule in order to improve. In 1960, 3 years before their first album, Please Please Me, they moved from Liverpool, England to Hamburg in Germany to play live concerts for experience, and more importantly, to practice. They were paid $3.50 per day. They worked 7 days a week playing in the city's music clubs. They played from 8.30-9.30pm, 10.00-11.00, 11.30-12.30, and finally on stage again at 1.00 until 2.00am for a final stint of the night! This routine continued for 2 years. They lived in awful conditions, but life revolved around their practice. I'm sure you'll agree this was quite a leap of faith for a group who had not yet made an album.

The Beatles steadily improved during their time in Hamburg. Paul McCartney remembers their progress: "We got better and better and other groups started coming to watch us". They had turned themselves into a leading group, even before they felt they were ready to release their music to the world. Patiently, they did not commit their music to record (which lasts forever) until they felt they were completely ready.

Without a doubt, they notched up their 10,000 hours early in their careers... and it paid off. As we all know, they went on to become the most successful rock group in history.

PEARLY GATES

Bill Gates

At an early age Bill Gates showed an interest in computers. In 1968, at the age of 13 he gained access to a high school computer. He practiced programming relentlessly and soon wrote a program for the game Tic-Tac-Toe (Noughts And Crosses) in basic computer language that allowed users to play against the computer. Remember this was in 1969, when computers and programming were very new and extremely basic compared to today's mind-blowing machines. During these early years Gates also developed a payroll program and also a scheduling program for the school. In 1970, at the age of 15 he officially had a business and developed a program that monitored traffic patterns in Seattle. He was paid $20,000 for this and his career went on from here.

It seems quite obvious that this dedicated, deliberate practice Bill Gates put in during his teens and early twenties, he had notched up his 10,000 hours before he turned 25. Bill was able move forward using his learned expertise to set up the company Microsoft and become the richest man on the planet.

EVERY PICTURE TELLS A STORY

Michelangelo

The most famous painter to have ever lived. Was he just 'lucky' to be born at the time of The Renaissance in Italy, the greatest ever era of painting and sculpture? Definitely his environment inspired him, but he put in his hours too. His commitment to art and sculpture at an early age led him to be somewhat of a social outcast, a label which remained with him for the majority of his life. He produced two of the most recognized and influential sculptures ever made – the Pietà and David, both before the age of 30! This was incredibly young for such achievement and recognition in his field during this era.

He was volunteered to paint the Sistine Chapel by several fellow artists of a similar age, one being the famous Raphael. They too were incredibly prominent artists of the time, but they felt the task of fresco painting the ceiling of The Sistine Chapel was one doomed to certain failure. Due to their jealousy and dislike of Michelangelo, they had the Pope select him to do it. Michelangelo had previously spoken of his disregard for painting (even though he could do it extremely well), but when asked by Pope Julias II to carry out the painting of the now great chapel, he couldn't refuse. At this stage of his life Michelangelo was obviously an incredible artist who had by far surpassed his 10,000 hours, but...

Fresco was new to Michelangelo. Fresco is a technique of mural painting executed upon freshly-laid, or wet plaster. He hired top apprentices to paint the ceiling. He would watch them all day. Months went by until one day he locked them out and never let them back into the chapel. He knocked down their work and started anew. He practiced and practiced until he felt he was ready. Michelangelo then began, working almost every hour of every day, rarely stopping to eat or sleep. He wouldn't leave the room for months at a time. The ceiling took him 4 years to complete. For anyone who is lucky enough to have seen the Sistine Chapel ceiling, hopefully you will also have had the art explained to you by an expert tour guide. The ceiling art work is made up of many different sections each depicting a different scene from the Bible's 'Book of Genesis'. You can identify the sections he painted first, and then as he worked from section to section through time, you can clearly see a change in style and quality. With every hour he spent on this artwork, you can see how he adapted his technique and became better and better. It's a wonderful illustration of improvement attained through deliberate practice.

"If people knew how hard I worked to get my mastery, it wouldn't seem so wonderful at all."

MICHELANGELO

Other modern day cases:

Beyoncé – along with 3 or 4 friends, they were all pushed hard by Beyoncé's father to practice in order to become a successful singing group. These girls practiced every day after school throughout their teen years. When they were signed by Columbia Records in 1997 to make an album as the group Destiny's Child, even though still young they were already approaching their 10,000 hours of practice (Beyoncé was 16 at this time). By the time they were late teens they had already become experts when other girl bands were just starting out.

These girls in Destiny's Child already knew their strengths. They knew what each individual member brought to the group, they knew how to dance, how to sing, how to perform, and they knew how they wanted to sound as a group. We know they went on to achieve great success in the pop charts and now Beyoncé has become one of the most popular, most recognized female singers of the last decade.

Tiger Woods – There's a TV clip of Tiger Woods when he was 2 years old (yes 2!) on The Mike Douglas Show. He stepped up, swung his golf club competently with nice technique, and hit the ball further than my wife could! Everybody in the audience thought this was funny and cute, but it was far more. This was the start of a love affair with the sport, which led to hours of practice from an unprecedented early age. Obviously with his commitment to practice, he went on to reach a standard of golf never seen before. What he also did differently was to put an emphasis on physical fitness. Fitness had never been considered essential for golf players before this, golf was all about technique. Since Tiger, most golf players now spend hours in the gym as well as on the golf course.

Becoming an expert so early in his life enabled Tiger to push the boundaries and change public conception of what the sport involves. He was a true pioneer of the sport.

Venus and Serena Williams – the two sisters spent all their early years on the tennis court. Like Tiger had done just a few years before, Venus changed public opinion about her sport. She brought a power to the tennis court never seen before in the women's game. She went on to win many majors and looked unstoppable until her younger sister came along to challenge her. Serena has surpassed her sister to become the greatest female tennis player of all time.

Mark Zuckerberg – the Facebook man was introduced to computer programming at the age of 11. His dad helped him by teaching him basic programming and later hired a private tutor to teach Mark about software development. Even in his early teens he was described by his tutor as a "prodigy". He quickly developed a software program to help his Dad's dental practice. This allowed all computers between the house and dental office to communicate with each other. This was considered a primitive version of AOL's Instant Messenger which was released the following year.

He spent many, many hours in his early teens developing computer software, especially communication tools and games. During his high school years he built a music player that could learn the users listening habits. Even before he was 20 Mark was already well on his way to completing his 10,000 hours.

Michael Jackson – forced to practice with his brothers from a very early age by Joe, their domineering father, Michael quickly became a childhood prodigy. He made his professional debut at the age of 5, and began his solo career when he was just 13 years of age. Very early in life he learned what his strengths were as a performer. At the age of 21 he released the album 'Off The Wall' which would kick start his superstardom. Then followed a string of albums considered to be among the greatest ever made, not to mentioning developing the world famous 'moonwalk'.

This magical 10,000 hour theory certainly does seem compelling, and is a good measure to work from. These examples are exceptional. In the majority of the mentioned cases they have managed to amass their 10,000 hours before the age of 20. This is not necessarily a pre-requisite of success, it undoubtedly helps but is not essential. It is possible to reach a high level at a young age but continue to learn on the job to achieve expert status.

I also believe business doesn't necessarily have to follow the same path as sport. All the same factors contribute to success (discipline, effort, goals and knowing ones strengths), that is a definite; but businesses can start from a place based more on personality strengths. You can be more patient with your time frame of achieving an expert level of skill and application. Whereas sport requires a higher level of physical prowess at a younger age. This is obvious when you think that the life span of a professional sportsman's playing career is much shorter. A sports career at the highest level is generally limited to between 20 and 35 years of age. Business caries no such limits.

The 10,000 Hour Rule is more definitive when talking about the arts, ie. sport and music. It is easier to quantify hours of physical training in a specific field, as opposed to business where many skills could have been transferred from similar jobs or tasks.

Knowing though, the amount of hours and effort sports stars put in to achieve excellence in their trade, any 'regular person' in any 'regular job' should ask themselves, if Roger Federer, Serena Williams, David Beckham and Michael Jordan are willing to put that amount of effort and practice into their trade, why shouldn't I?

I would also like to add; several of the examples above had especially forceful fathers which I do not condone. Supportive parents are unquestionably a wonderful thing, and without them it would be almost impossible to succeed as a top sportsman; but particularly forceful parents rarely achieve the desired result. For these cases, and in particular the extreme case of Joe Jackson, there will be thousands of others where it has actually driven the child away from success, especially in the long term. There are several books out there on how to be a good sports parent so I don't need to go into that!

AGE IS NOTHING BUT A NUMBER

"Age is no barrier. It's a limitation you put on your mind…"

JACKIE JOYNER-KERSEE

As promised here's a look at some cases where persistence and 'life experience' paid off and success was achieved much later in life. These offer an example that business success does not have to follow the same rigid path of 10,000 hours in a particular skill which is required for sport. Sport practice must be deliberate from a relatively young age, whereas in business, practice hours can start out 'less deliberate', and life experience definitely can help, before making the decision to narrow ones field and become more specifically deliberate. Every job, every task completed throughout our lives, is another lesson learned.

A MARRIAGE MADE IN HEAVEN

Vera Wang had been a fashion editor at Vogue magazine for 17 years, and then 2 years at Ralph Lauren. At the age of 40, after almost 20 years working in fashion, she decided she had gained enough experience, know-how and expertise from the fashion industry, that she resigned to become an independent bridal wear designer; her first job was to commission her own wedding dress! A year later she opened her first bridal boutique.

IT'S A FUNNY THING SHOW BUSINESS

At the age of 15, Jacob Cohen began to write for stand-up comedians, and soon began to perform himself under the name Jack Roy. After 20 years of struggling, he realized he had more chance of success if he created an image for himself; an on-stage persona audiences could relate to and would separate him from other similar comedy acts. He created *Rodney Dangerfield* – a character for whom nothing goes right. He received his big break on the Ed Sullivan show when he was 46. He went on to have an extremely successful stand-up comedy and acting career.

THE EVOLUTION OF SUCCESS

Charles Darwin was 50 years old when he published 'The Origin of the Species'. He had begun investigating his (at the time) widely disputed theory of natural selection 21 years earlier!

A GAP IN THE MARKET

Donald Fisher first owned a business renovating hotels before buying a hotel in Sacramento. He leased some retail space on the hotel ground floor to Levi Strauss & Co. After a bad experience with limited Levi stock he and his wife opened a store selling Levi jeans, along with music records and tapes. A few years later, Fisher and his wife set up the Gap label in 1972, when Donald was 44.

THE WRITING'S ON THE WAL-MART

Sam Walton had a series of jobs before joining the US military. In 1945, after leaving the military, Walton took over management of his first variety store at the age of 26. With the help of a $20,000 loan from his father-in-law, plus $5,000 he had saved from his time in the Army, Walton purchased a Ben Franklin variety store in Newport, Arkansas. The store was a franchise of the Butler Brothers chain. Walton pioneered many concepts that became crucial to his success. Walton made sure the shelves were consistently stocked with a wide range of goods. His second store, the tiny "Eagle" department store, was down the street from his first Ben Franklin and next door to its main competitor in Newport.

Walton was then met with several setbacks, but he continued in the shop trade and constantly found ways to prosper through adversity. Over the next 15 years he and his brother owned 16 small stores. Sam was 44 when he opened his first Wal-Mart store.

A RECIPE FOR SUCCESS

It was after meeting her would-be husband, Paul, who was brought up in a family very interested in food and cooking, that **Julia Child**'s path toward the culinary world began. As a married couple they moved to Paris where Julia had many life changing meals in restaurants. She attended the famous Le Cordon Bleu cooking school. Soon after she and a few friends began a cooking school for American women living in Paris. The now famous TV chef, didn't have her first published cookbook released until she was 39, and she didn't appear on TV until she was 51.

YOU PLAY THE WAY YOU PRACTICE

"Quality is never an accident. It is always the result of intelligent effort."

JOHN RUSKIN

Now we know how much practice is required to become a master, and we know that the practice must be purposeful, deliberate and goal orientated, but then there's the final factor of practice – ***HOW TO PRACTICE.***

In the book 'So Good They Can't Ignore You', author Cal Newport says that what makes ridiculously successful people so successful is they're experts at practicing — they can push themselves to the exact limit of their skillset and thus expand their abilities day after day. If we're not expanding ourselves in such a fashion — called *'deliberate practice'* — we'll never be ridiculously successful.

> *"I feel that luck is preparation meeting opportunity."*

OPRAH WINFREY

I don't want to dwell on how to practice as this is specific to each individual in every possible activity, but as I have earlier stated, 'deliberate practice' is a commitment. It involves thought and a set of goals. It needs to be as specialised as possible to achieve maximum results (a super-strength?). It requires results testing, feedback and analysis (the Feedback Loop). Without continually monitoring progress, practice will become increasingly aimless, less deliberate, and hours spent will not achieve improvement (like we saw with driving). If this feedback loop is ever broken, we are then wasting our time.

Balance is a key factor of any training regime. Do not over-train and do not under-train. Not only must practice be deliberate, but it must also be useful to the individual – training needs to be personal; catering to the individual's strengths and needs. Practicing the wrong things certainly won't help.

To continuously maintain 'deliberate practice' throughout ones career is very difficult, but it is what separates fleeting success stories from the truly successful who achieve longevity.

WHITE MEN CAN'T JUMP

"Standing tall has nothing to do with height."

UNKNOWN

Many would argue that 10,000 hours does not guarantee success, there needs to be some genetic help too. For example we could say; the reason four-time NBA scoring champion Kevin Durant is un-guardable is because of his commitment to practice, but also because he has a 7'2" wingspan paired with a 6'9" height. Certain activities require specific physical traits. We are highly unlikely to be a champion basketball player if we are only 5'8" tall, in the same way we're going to find it difficult to be a champion sumo wrestler if we are naturally skinny!

However, many people in the world thrive on defying common convention or public opinion (for example; one of the greatest soccer players of all-time is Argentinian Diego Maradona who is only 5'5"; and Floyd Mayweather Jr. at only 5'8" is considerably shorter than the opponents he fought… and he has never lost a professional fight!). Genetic factors are not a guarantee of failure, but they have to be a consideration if we are likely to achieve greatness. I would say if genetic factors could be a major factor working against our success then we have not played to our strengths in the first place. We would have chosen the wrong activity for our personal attributes. We must play to our strengths. These strengths start with genetic factors such as height, and personality traits. It is a skill to choose the ultimate activity for us to dedicate our time to.

I do not in any way want to discourage people from doing anything. I believe if we put our minds to it we can achieve almost anything. It depends what level of success we are after. Success is achieving levels we know are extremely difficult to reach for ourselves personally, and maybe others even said they were impossible. For some, success is to become the absolute world's best, and this can only be done if we are physically the right fit.

Not many jobs actually require a particular physical appearance but it's definitely worth bearing in mind. It was most definitely a factor which made it unlikely for me to become a top goalkeeper in the English Premiership soccer league, even though I lived in one of the most famous soccer cities in the world (Manchester).

The beauty of business is - it is not affected by physical factors such as weight or height. Physically, any size will do.

BOUNCE

"Every endeavour pursued with passion produces a successful outcome regardless of the result. For it is not about winning or losing – rather, the effort put forth in producing the outcome."

MATTHEW SYED

In 2010 Matthew Syed, a 3-time Commonwealth Gold Medalist table-tennis player, wrote a book called 'Bounce'. (We've already read an excerpt from his book in this Chapter). This book outlines the fact that talent is a myth and winners aren't born, but in fact they are made. This is not a new concept as we are now aware. He talks about the '10,000 Hour Rule' and 'deliberate practice'. Syed looks into real case studies with real results, not just over 4 weeks like Ericsson's violinists, but over years and decades. This book quickly became somewhat of a sportsman's bible, especially on the professional squash tour. Squash players at the elite level know of the incredible hard work, dedication and sacrifice it takes to become the best at any sport, and in particular a brutal sport like squash. I would recommend anyone to read this book, whatever your/their profession. I have passed this book on to squash players, tennis players, businessmen and teachers. They have all found it very useful in their profession and use it regularly in their teachings.

SO...

High achievers are not lucky. Winning the lottery is lucky. Hitting targets and reaching goals is down to one main ingredient above all...

The take-away key point from this Chapter is - EFFORT EFFORT EFFORT!

Every successful person in history; everybody who has committed to achieve their goals; has got there through sheer determination and effort. If you are not willing to put in the hours required, you will fail. Simple.

Let's recap once more:

-       Set yourself goals. Write them down. Assess and analyze along the way. This is very much linked to your deliberate practice.

-       What are your strengths? Know them and stick to them. Use them every day in everything you do.

These are what make you who you are. They will guide you and they will be ever-reliable, always there when you need them.

-       Do you have a secret weapon? To develop mastery of one skill or one subject is your aim. This is your super-strength and is what will make you stand out from any crowd. This is what can get you recognition in your field, and possibly fame and fortune.

Specialize, not compromise.

-       You must find a way to control your Chimp Brain; it will only hold you back if you don't.

- Without effort none of the above will ever materialize.

Now you know about the 10,000 Hour Rule. Dedication and discipline is what it takes to become an expert. There is no replacement – no shortcut.

Effort = Reward

"The man on top of the mountain didn't fall there."

VINCE LOMBARDI

8 BOUNCE BACK FROM A SETBACK

"Success is a result of good judgement – if you have good judgement and make the right decisions, you're going to succeed. Good judgement is the result of experience. Experience is often the result of bad judgement!"

TONY ROBBINS

Giving up on a goal because of a setback is like slashing your other three tyres because you got a flat!

Everyone on every professional journey will encounter setbacks, they are inevitable. What separates the weak from the strong is how they deal with any negative issues.

People I encounter in business and in sport tell me about setbacks which have recently happened to them and together we will look to find a solution. It is nice if we have someone we trust or a team of people to help, but often it comes down to us, and us alone to remain calm and rational in order to figure out the best possible way to respond during difficult times.

Obviously different professions and different problems require different actions; a setback for a lawyer in the middle of a big court case cannot have the same response as a tennis player who has just lost to their arch rival – I'm fairly sure practicing a sliced tennis serve will not help win that court case for the lawyer... but both situations do require some kind of response.

However, what has become obvious to me is that the attitude toward adversity is what counts for everything. Having the right mind-set after one of these setbacks is the difference between success and failure.

ACCEPTANCE IS MINDFULNESS

"Making your mark on the world is hard. If it were easy, everybody would do it. But it's not. It takes patience, it takes commitment and it comes with plenty of failure along the way."

BARACK OBAMA

No multinational CEO, sports star or leading hedge fund manager will ever say success came easily. Not only will they have put in their 10,000 hours of 'deliberate practice', but they will have had to deal with many complications along the way (some of which potentially career threatening). Setbacks happen to everyone. Any person we would consider successful or who we look up to for inspiration will have had many unforeseen problems. It is the way in which they viewed these problems that enabled them to move on and continue moving forward toward their goal. Whether it was Steve Jobs who was essentially sacked for a period not long after co-founding Apple; or Federer, who underwent possible career ending knee surgery in 2016; all successful people have approached setbacks with the same mindset – a positive one. Instead of simply accepting defeat, this positive growth mindset (mentioned in Chapter 7) empowered these people to actually prevail under duress and come flying out the other side of their troubles. These are the people who allow themselves to 'live and learn' (as opposed to those who 'live and complain').

A positive frame of mind is essential, but even before this positivity kicks in, where we would look for the good from every situation ("what doesn't kill us makes us stronger" and all that); the first step is ACCEPTANCE. Accepting that setbacks are normal and more likely – they are inevitable. Realizing *'I am not the first victim, and I will certainly not be the last'*. Nature can seem cruel; life is a process of overcoming obstacles, no matter how big or small. We overcome one obstacle while another one is waiting in the shadows. If we can accept this then we will be able to stay calm and rational during hard times, or even extreme adversity.

When a problem occurs nature will try to make us emotional, but we must not give in to our Chimp Brian – if we remain steady, measured and rational, we will find a solution. Use the mantra: *"Setbacks happen to everyone. I will come back wiser and stronger"* – and tell ourselves this over and over until we really believe it (and we should believe it because it's true!).

New York best-selling author Daniel G. Amen shows us there are "no straight-line graphs" on the path to success. No progress chart in history shows a perfect diagonal line which moves up rapidly as time passes. Progress has ups, downs and plateaus; peaks and troughs; good days, less good days and bad days. The ups inspire us of where we want to be, and the downs show us of the work still to be done.

When an issue arises or a setback comes our way, we are allowed to briefly feel discouraged, but we cannot wallow and we CANNOT QUIT. If we accept this has happened to us and understand it most likely won't be the last time either… we can and we will be able to move on from this. It's about taking time to think and assess the situation in order to calculate our next move.

A wise man knows that over time the highs continue to get higher and the lows become less low. Keep moving forward and we will continue to improve, heading toward our goal. Do not allow ourselves to be pegged back for long – be positive and be persistent.

Once we have accepted that troubles will emerge and setbacks will happen from time to time, we can face them with vigour and actually learn to enjoy the challenge. Through trials and tribulations, strength is found… and this strength leads us to self-improvement.

BOUNCE-BACK-ABILITY

~

RESPOND NOT REACT (Chimp Brain or Logical Brain)

"Any true champion can bounce back. That's what being a champion is: being able to deal with adversity and being able to bounce back."

FLOYD MAYWEATHER JR.

If and how we bounce back will determine if we go on to achieve our goals or not - whether we will be ranked up there with the professionally successful and admired, or whether we will be the type of person who is not professionally respected. Dawdlers and under-achievers make up the majority our population. We do not want to become just another statistic, do we?

A difficulty, issue, setback, problem, stumbling block, misfortune, roadblock, defeat, or whatever we want to call them; they are what's standing in the way of where we are now and where we want to be. We must bounce back. If we do not we will never come close to achieving our potential – and achieving our full potential is what we're trying to do here, it's the whole ethos of this book.

We cannot be somebody we're not. We play to our strengths, we bounce back when we need to, we make the most of what we have, and that can lead us to extraordinary things. Inside of us all, there is the potential to be great.

WHAT'S UP WHATSAPP?

A powerful story of bouncing back when close to quitting is the case of *Jan Koum*. Jan is the inventor of WhatsApp which in 2014 was sold to Facebook for over $19 billion! A pretty nice amount of money which almost could never have happened.

Here's a brief background of how WhatsApp came to be:

Koum was born in Kiev, Ukraine and moved to Mountain View, California at the age of 16 in 1992. They were a poor family who received government assistance to move into a small 2-bedroom flat. Koum quickly developed an interest programming. He worked many jobs to make ends meet, studied at San Jose State University and joined a hacking group (incidentally where he met Napster co-founder Sean Fanning).

After many years working for Yahoo! he and another colleague, Brian Acton, formed a close friendship. The two even took a year out, travelling around South America together with money they had saved from their time at Yahoo!. In 2009 Jan bought his first Apple iPhone and recognized an opportunity with the recently released App Store. He knew apps would soon spawn a whole new industry and he wanted to take advantage of it before it was too late. Koum had an idea to share the "status" of each individual in a person's phone book; for example if they were on a call, or out to lunch, at the gym or they have low battery. After many trials it developed into a messaging service, particularly good for sharing photos, and all for free without network costs, no matter where in the world the users were.

Early WhatsApp versions kept crashing or getting stuck, and when good friend and mentor Alex Fishman installed it on his phone, only a handful of the hundreds of numbers in his address book had also downloaded it. Over dinner Fishman went over the problems, Koum listened intently and took notes. The following month after a game of Ultimate Frisbee with Acton, Koum expressed his frustration of technical issues which were proving hard to fix. He went on to grudgingly admit he should probably give up and start looking for another job. Acton was shocked and replied: "You'd be an idiot to quit now. Give it a few more months."

And so he did. Together they worked though the issues and got WhatsApp up and running successfully. Once it was glitch-free, the app was soon generating great attention, and all without advertising (Jan Koum doesn't morally believe in it). Download and user numbers were increasing massively every week and before long, in 2012 it caught the attention of

Facebook owner, Mark Zuckerberg… Then as we say, the rest is history.

We could conclude that Jan Koum was lucky to have such a supportive friend who believed in him and his product, so much so that he simply wouldn't allow him to quit when the going got tough. Even so, the message is clear – the message of not giving up in times of adversity. Believe in ourselves and our abilities. Koum had shown great entrepreneurship with his idea and he had the technical skills to make it work. We can all see it would have been crazy if he had not continued on when he encountered the first major setback, especially after making it that far already.

BRUSHED OFF

In 1956 Andy Warhol literally couldn't give his work away. On October 18th the artist received a very polite letter from the Museum of Modern Art declining a drawing in which he had donated to the museum. Today, the MoMA owns 168 pieces of art by Warhol.

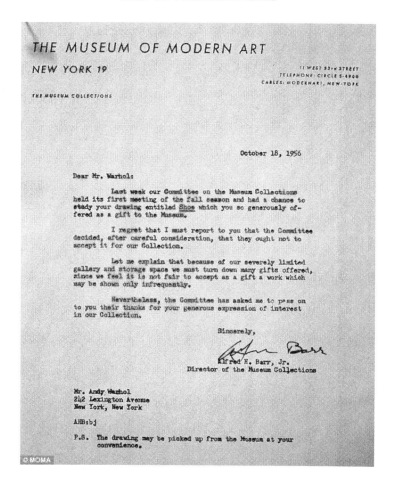

THE MUSEUM OF MODERN ART

NEW YORK 19

11 WEST 53rd STREET
TELEPHONE: CIRCLE 5-8900
CABLES: MODERNART, NEW-YORK

THE MUSEUM COLLECTIONS

October 18, 1956

Dear Mr. Warhol:

Last week our Committee on the Museum Collections held its first meeting of the fall season and had a chance to study your drawing entitled Shoe which you so generously offered as a gift to the Museum.

I regret that I must report to you that the Committee decided, after careful consideration, that they ought not to accept it for our Collection.

Let me explain that because of our severely limited gallery and storage space we must turn down many gifts offered, since we feel it is not fair to accept as a gift a work which may be shown only infrequently.

Nevertheless, the Committee has asked me to pass on to you their thanks for your generous expression of interest in our Collection.

Sincerely,

Alfred H. Barr, Jr.
Director of the Museum Collections

Mr. Andy Warhol
242 Lexington Avenue
New York, New York

AHB:bj

P.S. The drawing may be picked up from the Museum at your convenience.

© MOMA

LACK OF MATERIAL FROM THE MATERIAL GIRL

It seems almost impossible to imagine but there was a time when Madonna was just another singer with a demo tape hoping to get a record deal. Her manager at the time, Alec Head sent a demo tape to Millennium Records in the early 80's and received a rejection letter back from then executive Jimmy Lennor which said: "In my opinion, the only thing missing from this project is the material... I do not feel that she is ready yet, but I do hear the basis for a strong artist. I will pass for now, but I will wait for more."

Soon after, Madonna signed to Sire record label and released her first album, 'Madonna', which was followed in 1984 by her hugely popular second album, 'Like a Virgin'. She is now the most successful female artist of all time.

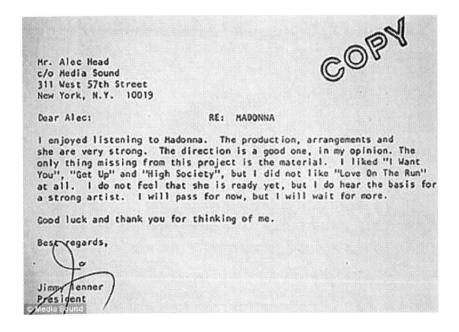

Mr. Alec Head
c/o Media Sound
311 West 57th Street
New York, N.Y. 10019

Dear Alec: RE: MADONNA

I enjoyed listening to Madonna. The production, arrangements and she are very strong. The direction is a good one, in my opinion. The only thing missing from this project is the material. I liked "I Want You", "Get Up" and "High Society", but I did not like "Love On The Run" at all. I do not feel that she is ready yet, but I do hear the basis for a strong artist. I will pass for now, but I will wait for more.

Good luck and thank you for thinking of me.

Best regards,

Jimmy Ienner
President

WITH OR WITHOUT RSO RECORDS

U2 are rock 'n' roll's biggest band, who in one year make more money than most countries' gross national income. But there was a time when Paul Hewson (Bono), Dave Evans (The Edge), Adam Clayton and Larry Mullen Jr were just 4 teenagers trying to get noticed in the music world. The group sent several demo tapes to record labels and one generic rejection letter received back from Bono in 1979 read:

'Dear Mr. Hewson,

Thank you for submitting your tape of 'U2' to RSO, we have listened with careful consideration, but feel it is not suitable for us at present.'

RSO Records made the fateful decision to pass on signing U2. Never heard of RSO Records? That's because they've been out of business for three decades!

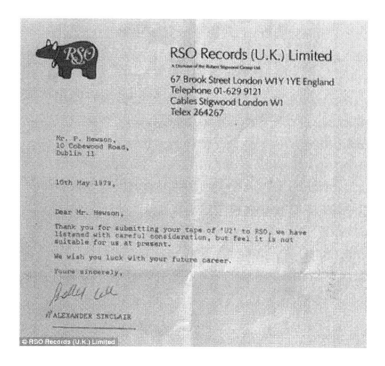

THE POWER OF POSITIVE

"A pessimist sees the difficulty in every opportunity; an optimist sees the opportunity in every difficulty."

WINSTON CHURCHILL

OK, now we have acceptance that setbacks happen to everyone and now let's imagine we're in a situation where it's happened to us. We are in complete control of how we perceive every problem that comes our way. When something bad or unexpected happens, we decide what it means for us and our careers. Is this the end or something we can learn from? Is this the worst thing to ever happen to us or just a bump in the road?

You need a POSITIVE GROWTH MIND-SET.

There is a positive and negative way to look at any situation. We do not have to be an outrageous optimist, but we must remain calm and balanced and look for the way to move forward. There is always a way. Positivity is not being unrealistic or delusional, but instead it is accepting the facts and still having the desire to move forwards, not backwards from any situation.

STEP 1 TO POSITIVITY. *JUST A HICCUP*

A setback is merely a hiccup, or a bump in the road. It may momentarily slow us down but it is <u>not preventative</u> to our goal.

A defeat can be slightly more extreme. Any loss is hard to take initially, whether we have lost out on winning a business deal, or we have lost in the final of the US Open. Losses always give us much to learn from, we just have to take a step back. Step away from the raw emotion and we will be able to see the lessons to be learned… ask ourselves: *Why did that outcome happen? In hindsight what could I could have done differently? Did I play to my strengths? Or maybe I simply need to go away, knuckle-down and improve my skills a little more?*

STEP 2 TO POSITIVITY. *CONTROL THE CHIMP*

The normal reaction to problems is to cast blame. Chimp comments will kick in; blaming our boss for putting us in that situation; feeling frustrated at the company for not seeing how amazing we are; cursing the traffic for making us late for our appointment; attributing losing the match to the unfavourable weather conditions; or having the opinion of 'nobody sold any products today so why should I have?'

We need acceptance, and the sooner the better. Accept it happened and begin to analyze why it happened while it's still fresh in our minds. Seek information and feedback to look for ways to improve our current position.

Anger is another reaction which is closely related to blame. Anger at ourselves or at somebody else.

Problems will make us initially emotional. Move away from emotionally led reactions as soon as possible. We need to be calm in order to consider and reflect before we can plan how to move forward and what to do next.

STEP 3 *TO POSITIVITY. ANALYSIS*

Hopefully now we are calm and have realized that this setback is not the end of the world. Now it is time to begin planning our response.

Do not panic and be willing to give ourselves time. *Did we play to our strengths?* There must either be a better way to apply our strengths to avoid this same situation occurring again, or we need to make one of our strengths even stronger to create a super-strength. Never lose faith in what we have to offer. Our strengths are what can make us great. We are unique. We potentially have everything we need.

STEP 4 *TO POSITIVITY. APPLY FEEDBACK*

Use all the feedback we have gathered and apply it to create our action plan of what to do next. Be willing to adjust our method but never change our end goal.

"Difficulties mastered are opportunities won."

WINSTON CHURCHILL

SO...

The message is a clear one. Don't give up when times are hard. You have set yourself a goal which you know is right for you and you know you can achieve it. You know setbacks are likely to happen somewhere before you reach your end goal, they happen to everyone. It would be incredibly naïve to think it would be plain sailing the whole way. Successful people accept setbacks and think of the best way to move forward and learn from them.

With each Chapter you've learned the following:

-    Techniques on how to set a goal which you will see though to the very end.

-    The best way to self-improvement is to follow your strengths. Be aware of what you are good at and use these skills to increase performance.

It is possible these strengths will make you realize that a change of direction is required to best use your greatest attributes.

-    Once you are playing to your strengths and seeing the benefits every day (which you undoubtedly will), you can begin to focus more and more on your strongest skill. Turn something good into something great.

-    Don't let irrational thoughts get in the way of progress.

-    Never shy away from putting in the hard graft. Some days you will not want to put in maximum effort, but force yourself for these difficult days will build character and feel even more rewarding. There is no substitute for effort and experience.

-    Be aware that difficulties will arise. Do you have what it takes to bounce back?

When difficulties occur, do not react emotionally. Control your Chimp Brian and your negative thoughts. Respond positively and treat any setback as a challenge. With the right response you will move forwards and you will learn from them. With time you may even enjoy these challenges!

"A setback is never a bad experience, just another one of life's lessons."

RICHARD BRANSON

9 ANYONE FOR CONSULTANCY?

"Instead of waiting for a leader you can believe in, try this: Become a leader you can believe in."

STAN SLAP

Consultant: A professional who offers expert advice. They have a particular area of expertise.

We are living in an age where people crave expertise, and they are willing to pay top dollar for expert advice. We've discussed the importance of playing to our strengths, specializing where possible and looking to create a super-strength; so if we do have the right skill set then naturally we should have a look into consultancy.

NOT SO COMMON SENSE

"It is a thousand times better to have common sense without education than to have education without common sense."

ROBERT INGERSOLL

To be a consultant we need an in-depth knowledge of a certain subject, no matter how small or specialized ie. we must be considered an expert or have expert credentials in our chosen field whatever that may be. In fact, the more specialized our area of expertise the better.

Consultancy requires a confident individual who can sell their skills to other people or companies. The consultant must be able to convince the client that they need the skills and knowledge which the consultant can offer, and with their help the client will see dramatically improved results. Basically every consultant not only must have a specialist subject but must also be a salesman!

The personality traits/'Talent Themes' a consultant requires is to be an Achiever obviously, and ideally all of the 'Commitment Themes', particularly 'Self-Assurance'. If we are to be capable of selling what we have to offer we would need to back ourselves 100%. To have the confidence to sell what we are offering and to tell people or companies that our knowledge will help their business thrive. If *you* feel you possess these attributes, think seriously about the consultancy market available to you.

There is one more vital ingredient needed to become a consultant. An area of which is worryingly absent in the business world – *common sense!* It's amazing how uncommon 'common sense' actually is. *Newsflash:* Common sense is not directly linked to intelligence. There are lots of intelligent people in the world with no common sense.

What makes a great consultant is when somebody can fuse their expertise with common sense and apply it to the workplace. A close friend of mine began his career as a school teacher. He became disillusioned with the lack of everyday common sense being applied by the staff, the educational leaders and the decision makers for the school. He decided his strengths did not lie in being a class room teacher, but instead he decided he could use his in-depth understanding of the English educational system for another purpose. (After a decade of teaching he had acquired extensive knowledge of how schools function. He knew about the government initiatives and expectations imposed on schools, and along with this, his wife was also a Deputy-Head teacher at another school). With his comprehension of day-to-day schooling coupled with his straight talking nature and common sense, he knew there was a market for him to become an educational consultant. His job is to talk to school principals and advise them how to apply what resources they have and apply them to new and current government schemes with the goal of helping the pupils realize their full potential ie. the aim is to improve overall school grades.

The majority of advice to schools he considers to be no more than common sense. He is a modest man and I'm sure his assessment of his skills is somewhat simplified, but he is also completely correct. Application of expertise requires common sense to achieve significant results. There are many businesses, schools, associations and people out there who have a good product, good resources or good ideas but are lacking the know-how or skill to bring them all together to produce meaningful results. They need a guide, a helping hand, and this is where consultants come in.

TRUST ME, I'M A CONSULTANT

"An expert is one who knows more and more about less and less."

NICHOLAS M. BUTLER

If you feel you have prowess in a speciality subject; you have the desired personality traits; and you can apply all this with basic common sense - then you have what it takes to offer consultancy. You'd be amazed how many people actually need what you have to offer. All you have to do is to find the right channel to showcase your specialized skills. You have a USP and people *will* pay for it. Be confident. Be bold. Sell yourself.

Expertise is difficult to gain. As we know it takes a huge commitment; hours upon hours of effort with 'dedicated practice'. However once we have the skills or possibly the official qualification needed to demonstrate our expert status, the job is not yet done. Convincing people of our skills is the easy part. People can recognize expertise, but to convince people that they are lacking in common sense or the vision to apply their work is considerably more of a challenge – **common sense is something that everyone needs, few have, and none think they lack.**

First time customers buy what you know. Repeat customers buy who you are.

If we do consider ourselves as a consultant, how we come across to our clients is absolutely key. Personal and professional manner, on top of expertise is how a person can financially survive as a consultant. 'Experts' know they have specialized skills; the client knows the 'expert' has specialized skills... but what makes a 'true expert' is the application and delivery.

"If you can't explain it simply, you don't understand it well enough."

ALBERT EINSTEIN

A successful consultant is someone who can apply their specific skills to new situations and can deliver their ideas to their client. They can relay their expertise to their customer in a language which they understand. A consultant should speak the clients language and not make the client learn theirs. Ideas not only need to be capable of producing results but they must also come with clear instructions.

Fusing expertise with common sense and producing positive results builds up client-consultant trust. Common sense and trust are the real skills required for this professions. If you feel you can deliver these then consultancy could be a great opportunity for you to play to your strengths.

If a person truly can play to their strengths and help people on a daily basis, then what better profession than consultancy.

HIDDEN IN PLAIN SIGHT

"Knowledge is power. The more knowledge, expertise and connections you have, the easier it is for you to make a profit at the game of your choice."

STUART WILDE

Consultancy options are literally limitless. Remember general is no longer the future. Specialist subjects are the future, no matter how small or specialized. To narrow ones field of vision is the key to opening up ones field of opportunity.

Our world continues to move forward at a rate of knots with new technologies and concepts arriving all the time:

3D Printers that are capable of producing hamburgers, t-shirts, houses or even a perfectly functioning human organ;

Self-driving trucks which never need a 'toilet break' or 'snack stop';

Thanks to Tesla we will all soon be driving around in electric cars which outperform our current petrol and diesel engines;

Hot solar cells giving twice the efficiency as current solar panels;

Gene therapy with the potential to eradicate some diseases;

Agricultural drones increasing crop production;

Electrovibration technology is seen as the way forward in allowing us to really 'touch' different textures on our touch screens;

Hamwell's e-shower could potentially help alleviate the world's water crisis as it can recycle the water we're using in real time;

The new marketing idea of reducing sales options called 'constraint satisfaction', with the goal not to overwhelm the customer … the list could go on.

With these advancements come new opportunities. Each and every innovation requires expert teachers to bring them to the masses, thus creating new and wonderful consultancy job titles every time. I'm sure by now you get the message that if you have expert knowledge in a particular subject, consultation is a possible form of income for you. It does not always have to be your main source of income, but you could simply offer it as an additional service to people and companies who you have come to know who can benefit from your specific expertise.

We all should keep our eyes open to opportunities. Opportunities which may not be available now, or even exist now. As our skills improve on our path toward self-improvement and possible mastery, our demand and our value will also go up. We simply need to recognize the potential in consultancy, and it does not have to be here and now. There's no rush.

"Price is what you pay. Value is what you get."

WARREN BUFFETT

10 FINAL THOUGHTS

"Don't count the days, make the days count."

MUHAMMAD ALI

Remember: This book is about YOU, and how YOU can improve YOURSELF.

Wow, we've come a long way since Chapter 1. With everything you have learned now ask yourself this question: *If I could do anything what would it be?*

More often than not, people ask themselves this question when they are at a crossroads in their life, or more usually when they feel low and are looking for a way out of whatever it is which is making them feel sad (usually work!). But in fact, this is a question which should only be asked when we feel strong and are in a positive frame of mind. We can only know our true desires when we are feeling confident; the best of who and what we are will rise up to the surface - this is the power of positivity.

Concentrating on what we are best at carries a far greater impact than people first imagine. We cannot underestimate the mental role our strengths play in our life. Humans are happiest when we feel in control. The sense of control creates a comfortable environment around us; an environment in which we can flourish. When we do flourish, we can achieve great things.

Doing what we are good at makes us happy. Doing what we are good at will create an environment for further improvement. These personal strengths are what can help us reach the tremendous heights which we are individually capable of, even if we do not believe it or know what they are yet.

I sincerely hope you have been inspired by the facts and the real life examples in this book. Always remember - you are unique. Please take inspiration from others but do not feel the need to compare yourself to others. You have the power to be a great achiever. You have the power to increase your productivity in any situation. Embrace who you are and what you are best at. It's a fun journey, so go on, don't be shy!

Before you go let's briefly revisit what we've covered (with the aid of some simple diagrams):

TAKE CONTROL – SET YOUR GOAL

Hope is not a strategy.

If you didn't know it already, I'm fairly sure you do now: Setting goals greatly increases your chances of success. Writing down these goals further increases your chances.

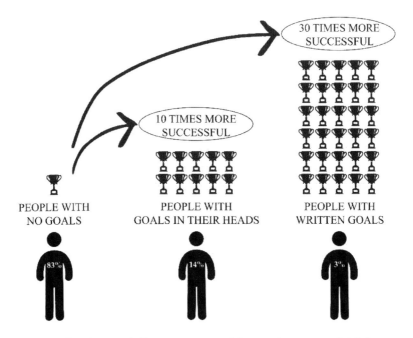

Goals must be clear and direct; use no ambiguous language which is open to interpretation. Goals should be broken down and measurable. We should make ourselves accountable and value any feedback offered. Celebrate successes.

These are the tried and tested steps to achieving any goal.

DO WHAT YOU DO BEST

Go where your strengths lead you.

Take a long, positive look at yourself. Be honest and write down what you are best at. What are your personality strengths? What are your skills? What areas do you have above average knowledge? Do you have any physical strengths?

Every person is unique. Every person must have answers to the above questions, other than "none"! Reflect on what you have done well in the past and look to copy it or use that method again.

We need to find ways to actively apply our strengths in every situation possible. If you are currently not doing this then that is why you are not progressing. Consider how you can apply your strengths to every task; there is always a way. By applying what we're good at, our strengths will naturally improve and we will become stronger, more productive, more efficient and more valuable.

'Harmonious passion' is a fancy phrase to describe the autonomous process of selecting what we naturally enjoy. We enjoy doing what we are good at. Psychologist Robert Vallerand says feeling a harmonious passion for a task – that is, our interest in it is deep enough to be part of our identity – can greatly improve our performance. If we feel we are doing something that reflects our feelings and values, it adds another layer of engagement, as it involves us on a deeper level.

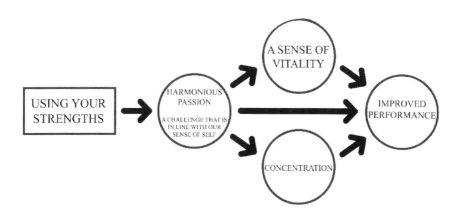

Playing to our strengths without a doubt makes us happier and more productive. The 'halo effect' is a psychological concept state where we make opinions about other people based on limited information. A US study confirmed that happy and warm people are generally seen as competent and trustworthy, therefore being in a happier mood at work could translate into better appraisals and higher pay.

Concentrate on applying all your strengths in order to show your true worth. By applying your strengths you can create any situation or environment into one in which you can thrive. Strengths will become stronger.

GOING FROM STRENGTH TO SUPER-STRENGTH

Why settle for good when you can have one skill which is great?

After isolating your strengths you'll be seeing results straight away and your confidence will soar.

The next step for us is to consider if we can develop one area into a super-strength. If "yes" then great. Hone in on this skill and work hard to perfect it. Then we build our strategy around creating our super-strength; use our other strengths to support our main weapon.

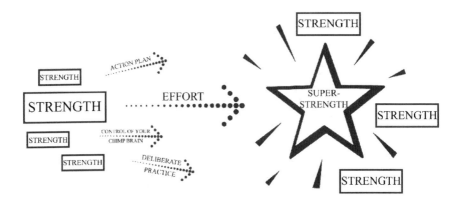

YOUR BEST FRIEND AND YOUR ENEMY

Your inner chimp must not sabotage your happiness and your success.

Our Chimp Brian allows us to feel the highs of success… and who doesn't want to feel that buzz when we're doing something well, or feel the delight when something good happens to us? Happiness is crucial to our existence, because after all, what is life without happiness. But… our Chimp Brain can be what prevents us from that very same success which we seek. Often our Chimp Brain is the reason why we fail, or never even make a start.

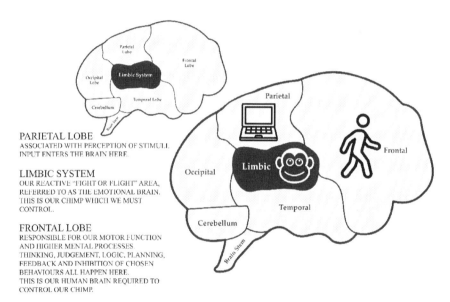

PARIETAL LOBE
ASSOCIATED WITH PERCEPTION OF STIMULI
INPUT ENTERS THE BRAIN HERE.

LIMBIC SYSTEM
OUR REACTIVE "FIGHT OR FLIGHT" AREA,
REFERRED TO AS THE EMOTIONAL BRAIN.
THIS IS OUR CHIMP WHICH WE MUST
CONTROL.

FRONTAL LOBE
RESPONSIBLE FOR OUR MOTOR FUNCTION
AND HIGHER MENTAL PROCESSES.
THINKING, JUDGEMENT, LOGIC, PLANNING,
FEEDBACK AND INHIBITION OF CHOSEN
BEHAVIOURS ALL HAPPEN HERE.
THIS IS OUR HUMAN BRAIN REQUIRED TO
CONTROL OUR CHIMP.

We must learn to process input with our Human Brain (Frontal lobe) in order to control our emotions to make measured decisions. It is these rational thoughts which lead us to the good choices we make; and good choices are essential when pursuing our goals. The chimp brain is pure passion, and in a pressure situation we must not react with emotion but respond with logic. Of course our emotions are essential; we do not want to become a robot, but we must control when our chimp is allowed out of its cage. If we do not control the door to the cage, irrational thoughts can cloud our judgement - we cannot waver in our commitment toward success.

ALL IN GOOD TIME

You are what you put in.

Is 10,000 hours of deliberate practice really worth our time? "Yes it is" is the simple answer. We must get it out of our heads that some people are just lucky or there is a super-fast route to achieving excellence. There is no hidden 'left before the traffic lights' to Success Street, no magic words like "abracadabra"; there's no secret shortcut we can take. Effort is what's required, and a lot of it. Anders Ericsson's violinists showed us that.

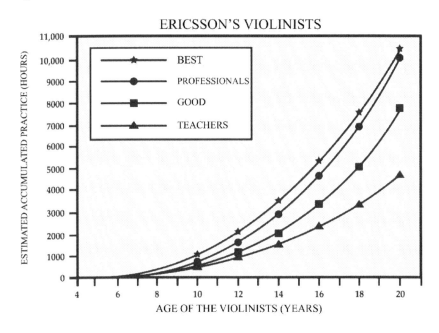

"It's a funny thing, the more I practice the luckier I get." - ARNOLD PALMER

We must understand though that there is a difference between excellence and success. It depends on how we judge success. Without a doubt, applying the methods in this book, by highlighting and playing to our strengths, we will see an almost instant impact. Our productivity and confidence will improve and will continue to do so due to a positive snowball effect. This self-improvement is most definitely a success, but is it the full success you are after, or simply the first step in your bigger plan?

To create mastery of a subject, or a super-strength skill, or to become one of the country's best; this requires a long term investment of effort and 10,000 hours is a good estimate of the time it will take. So now it is merely a question of honing in on our chosen practice. Decision is the key. Once we make the right choice for us and we have our action plan of how to reach excellence, there will be nothing stopping us.

10,000 hours is the equivalent of almost 3 hours 'deliberate practice' every single day for a decade. I know it sounds daunting but the chance is you are already well on your way to this figure. Hours do not have to be solely notched up on the practice court, or sat in front of the computer learning how to re-programme Microsoft Word, or dancing solo in front of a mirror; hours 'in the field' also count. Competitions, office hours solving problems or completing tasks, trying to win that big contract; any real life situations where we are applying our strengths and gaining experience all count, and will all be working toward our personal development, pushing us closer toward excellence and ultimately our end goal.

Effort = Reward

WILL YOU CRACK OR BOUNCE BACK?

When faced with adversity the weak wilt while the successful shine.

Setbacks will make us emotional. We have to practice to remain calm, and to keep our emotions balanced.

When a problem occurs we must not react in a hot-headed manner. Instead we need to take our time, accept what has happened and process the information logically. In every situation, keep calm and apply our strengths to find a solution – always working back to our action plan.

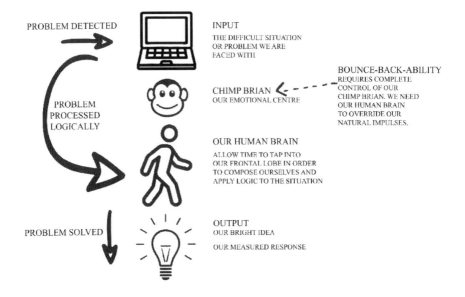

This is a vital skill which can be learned, and we will improve at it with experience. We mustn't allow ourselves to become just another under-achiever simply because we faced a tricky situation. Instead let us be one of the successful elite who tackle problems head-on and find a way to not only get through them, but to come out the other side stronger and empowered, with a heightened sense of purpose and an increased desire to succeed.

THE OVERLOOKED SENSE

Mastery plus common sense is a real superpower.

The last Chapter briefly addressed consultancy as a career option for anyone with two key components: An area of expertise, and common sense.

Both of these factors are essential to be a productive consultant, however it is not just consultancy which requires skill combined with common sense. Any successful entrepreneur, pioneer, business owner or consultant must know how to apply common sense to their application of skill. A person who cannot fuse the two, may go on to reach an extraordinary level of mastery but could never become a leader. It is the skill of applying expert knowledge to the world surrounding us, and to possess the ability to communicate that information to the people around us in the simplest possible manner. The people who prevail are those who can recognize opportunity, but not only that; they can also explain to the public why their product or service is so essential.

Never overlook the role common sense plays in our success.

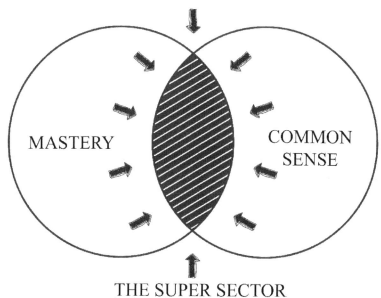

THE SUPER SECTOR
WITH BOTH MASTERY AND COMMON SENSE

*All diagrams in this book can be downloaded from my website www.andywhipp.com

ACKNOWLEDGEMENTS

My wife and my two daughters are the 3 people who make my life great. Helena is simply a fantastic person who I am lucky to be married to. Lucy and Alice are individually so different and so similar. They are best friends. We are all best friends. My three girls fill me with joy and happiness every single day. Everything I do, I do it for them.

There is no way I would have had a life at all similar to what I have had if it wasn't for my father. His support, his ethics and his humour will never be forgotten. I am completely the man I am because of him. Thanks Dad.

Reading an article many years ago by squash champ Nick Matthew, was when I first came across the concept of having a super-strength. It explained something in a simple, snappy phrase which I already believed in. Since that day it has been a main focus of mine. Nick has recently set up some 'Masterclass' coaching sessions at his home club in Sheffield where he talks about developing a super-strength to enhance ones squash ability. Nick is not only a great champion but he is a superb ambassador for squash. He is always appropriately funny and informative! His book 'Sweating Blood'; about life as a professional squash player, training and travelling playing the world tour; is a great read. It gives the unassuming an idea of how brutal it is to choose and succeed in any sport, particularly one as demanding as squash (which I am fully aware of as I sit here typing with sciatica, a tear in my calf muscle and another tear in my buttock, all from playing too much squash!).

Lawrence is a superb businessman and an inspiration to be around. He is very much a believer in me and my personality. Being around Loz is great fun. Our conversations cover the whole spectrum from utterly ridiculous to fascinatingly ponderous. He has been a great person to observe for this book.

Nadim, Ricardo and Richie are great friends who are always available any time I need some good advice, so a big thank you to those fellas.

I will always feel indebted to my coach throughout my teen years. Yawar was a super coach for me. He's a top guy and a great friend. I loved every single session we ever had. He facilitated my growth as a squash player and as a person. He was always happy to plan our sessions according to my strengths; which was basically running around as fast and hard as I could for an hour every week!

Everyone who I am close to who are involved in business and sport, has given me much food for thought. A mere few include; restauranteur Jobe who's an absolutely top man, Alan who is a leading businessman, has been extremely supportive in recent years, and world champion Laura who I would consider to be one of the most contemplative sports stars in the UK.

The first 'business' book I ever read was 'The Millionaire Messenger' by author, motivational coach and marketing expert Brendon Burchard. The book describes how almost anyone can use their life experiences to offer useful advice. It's an excellent read and most definitely provides necessary encouragement to any budding entrepreneur. I've mentioned 'Bounce' in this book, Matthew Syed certainly gives an interesting take on sport and business with all three of his books so far. The last book I read was 'Money: Master the Game' by Tony Robbins, which I loved even though it's about as heavy as a small child!

NOTES

Of course Google has been the go to search engine and Wikipedia has been of tremendous use to gain useful background knowledge before moving on to delve deeper through other sources.

1: Introduction

Success definition: Google online dictionary

2: Why Me?

Squash facts: England Squash, WSF, PSA, sweatband.com, townandcountrymag.com

"World's healthiest sport": Forbes Magazine 2003

UK Squash Circuit: The BSPA

AWsome Sports: bsports.co.uk

3: Fail To Plan, Plan To Fail

Chimp Brain: 'The Chimp Paradox – The Mind Management Programme' by Professor Steve Peters 2012

Deliberate practice: 'The Role Of Deliberate Practice in the Acquisition of Expert Performance' by K. Anders Ericsson 1993

European Journal of Social Psychology: sourced from the book 'Success – The Psychology of Achievement' by Deborah A. Olsen 2017

Goals: 'A Theory of Goal Setting and Task Performance' by Locke and Latham 1990

"Doing one's best": 'Toward a Theory of Task Motivation and Incentives' by Edwin 1968

Gail Matthews: Research into Goals conducted at Dominican University in 2015

4: Play To Your Strengths

Untapped/unlocked potential: 'Hidden Skills – Towards Maturity' research presented by Laura Overton 2008

Chimp Brian: 'The Chimp Paradox – The Mind Management Programme' by Professor Steve Peters 2012

Confidence attributes: thanks to Nora Bouchard 'Super Strengths in Real Life' 2014

Clifton's 'Now, Discover Your Strengths': Donald Clifton, Sally Byrne Woodbridge and Marcum Buckingham linked to the Gallup StrengthsFinder 2.0 with 34 "Talent Themes"

Lawrence Jones podcasts: available at lawrencejones.co.uk. Interviews with Steven Bartlett (CEO Social Change); Chris Percivil (medical service provider); Carrie Green (founder Female Entrepreneur Association); James Timpson (Timpsons shops owner); Richard Branson (Virgin).

Rafael Nadal: Wikipedia

Richard Branson on delegation: found at virgin.com/entrepreneur

School Principal job requirements: tes.com, Head Teacher Job Description

5: Super-Strengths

Elon Musk: Wikipedia

Study of 11,000 US scientists and engineers: 'Extreme Trust – Honestly as a Competitive Advantage' by Don Peppers and Martha Rogers 2012

Do Won Chang: Forbes profile

Guy Laliberté: Wikipedia

Richard Desmond: Wikipedia

Oprah Winfrey: Wikipedia

Under Armour: Stock information via The Motley Fool

The Body Shop: Wikipedia and The Guardian

6: The Commitment Commodity

Richard Branson hiring sportsmen: The Richard Branson at virgin.com

University of Scranton research: conducted by John C. Norcross in 2002

New Year's Resolutions: ComRes poll of resolutions

Chimp Brain: 'The Chimp Paradox – The Mind Management Programme' by Professor Steve Peters 2012

7: Effort = Reward

Ray Dalio: with the use of Wikipedia and a 2017 Tony Robbins interview on YouTube

Fixed vs Growth Mindset: 'Mindset – The New Psychology of Success' by Carol Dweck 2006

Rafael Nadal, Usain Bolt, Kobe Bryant: information from Wikipedia

'Bounce' by Matthew Syed: 2010

Andy Murray moved to Barcelona, Spain: Autobiography 'Hitting Back' 2008

'The 3

Hour Rule' and "deliberate practice": 'The Role Of Deliberate Practice in the Acquisition of Expert Performance' by K. Anders Ericsson 1993

Geoffrey Colvin: 'Talent is Overrated' 2008

Beatles in Hamburg: Wikipedia

Bill Gates: Wikipedia

Michelangelo: Vatican tours and Wikipedia

Beyoncé: Wikipedia

Tiger Woods: The Mike Douglas Show 1978

Mark Zuckerberg: Wikipedia

Michael Jackson: Wikipedia

Age is nothing but a number: Thanks to Inc.com and further information via Wikipedia

'So Good They Can't Ignore You': by Cal Newport 2012

8: Bounce Back From A Setback

Daniel Amen: author of 'Change Your Brain, Change Your Life' 1998

Jan Koum: Wikipedia and 'The Rags To Riches Tale' by Forbes writer Parmy Olson

Madonna, U2 and Andy Warhol rejection letters: Thanks to BBC Music and Mental Floss, and Daily Mail online for the pictures

9: Anyone For Consultancy?

Definition: Google online dictionary

New technologies: thanks to NewStatesman, MIT Technology Review and Forbes magazines.

10: Final Thoughts

Goals diagram: information from Naveen Raju 2015

Robert J. Vallerand: Professor Of Psychology at Université du Québec à Montréal

"Halo effect": Phrase first used by Edward Thorndike 1920. Research taken from 'Beauty and the Labor Market' by Hammeresh and Biddle 1994

Chimp Diagram: 'The Chimp Paradox – The Mind Management Programme' by Professor Steve Peters 2012

Ericsson's violinists diagram: Study by Ericsson, Krampe and Tesch-Römer 1993

INDEX

10,000 Hour Rule — 101-108, 109, 113, 114, 115, 118, 141-142

3D printing — 44, 133

Abraham Lincoln — 82 (quote)

Achiever Talent Theme — 41, 43-45, 47, 49, 50, 51, 53, 64, 65, 79, 130

Albert Einstein — 66 (quote), 132 (quote)

Alexander Pope — 35 (quote)

Amelia Earhart — 92 (quote)

Anders Ericsson — 101, 103, 103 (quote), 141

Andre Agassi — 90 (quote)

Andy Murray — 13, 100

Andy Warhol — 122

Antoine De Saint-Exupery — 26 (quote)

Arnie Sherr — 89 (quote)

Arnold Palmer — 141 (quote)

AWsome Sports Ltd — 5, 17

Barack Obama — 91 (quote), 118 (quote)

Barrie Davenport — 39 (quote)

Beyoncé — 106

Bill Gates — 104

blogging — 5, 69

'Bounce' book — 97-100, 114

Bradley Wiggins — 83 (quote)

Brian Tracy — 4, 22 (quote)

Bruce Lee — 102 (quote)

Cal Newport — 112

Carol Dweck — 92

Charles Darwin — 110

Chimp Brain — 18, 34, 83-88, 93, 94, 101, 115, 119, 120, 126, 128, 140

Clifton Strengths Finder — 40-47

Clifton's 'Talent Themes' — 40-51, 68, 130

confidence — 34-37, 39, 45, 46, 47, 53, 56-57, 60-62, 65, 74, 79, 87, 130, 139, 142

consultancy definition	129	Geoffrey Colvin	102
consultancy	129-134	goals diagram	19, 26, 137
Cyril Connolly	32 (quote)	goals	18-29, 36, 37, 38, 44, 45, 47, 52, 53, 54, 61, 62, 65, 78, 81, 82, 89, 108, 112, 115, 120, 136-137
Daniel Amen	119		
David Beckham	108		
deliberate practice	18, 101, 102-106, 109, 111-112, 114, 115, 118, 141-142		
		Goran Ivanisevic	71-73, 75
Diego Maradona	113	Greg Norman	73 (quote)
Do Wong Chang	70	growth (positive) mindset	92, 93, 118
Donald Clifton	40	Guinness	75
Donald Fisher	110	Guy Laliberte	70
Douglas Conant	88 (quote)	halo effect	138
Duncan Sheik	96 (quote)	Harbhajan Singh Yogi	56 (quote)
effort = reward	22, 59, 90-92, 115, 142	harmonious passion	138
		Henry Kissenger	29 (quote)
Eleanor Roosevelt	18 (quote)	Henry Whipp	10-11
Elon Musk	67 (quote)	Jackie Joyner-Kersee	109 (quote)
Elsie Larson	61 (quote)	Jan Koum	120-122
Elvis Presley	6	Jeff Gitmor	33 (quote)
European Journal of Social Psychology	20	Jennifer Lopez	48 (quote)
fixed mindset	92-93	Jessie J	31 (quote)
Floyd Meyweather Jr	113, 120 (quote)	Jiddu Krishnamurti	48 (quote)
		Jim Valvano	10 (quote)
Forbes	5 (quote)	John Ruskin	111 (quote)
Gail Matthews	23-25, 27	Jonah Barrington	5 (quote)

Jonathan Kemp	8-10, 12, 21
Julia Child	111
Karl Lagerfeld	34 (quote)
Kenneth Blanchard	81 (quote)
Kevin Durant	113
Kobe Bryant	97, 100
Lawrence Jones	21, 44, 53-55, 146
Locke and Lathan	21
Lou Holtz	3 (quote)
Madonna	123
Malcolm Gladwell	101
Manchester United	7, 9
Marcus Berrett	14, 16
Marcus Buckingham	40
Marilyn Vas Savant	59 (quote)
Mark Zuckerberg	43 (quote), 107, 122
Matthew Syed	97, 99-100, 114 (quote), 146
Maximizer Talent Theme	42, 45, 51, 53, 68
Michael Jackson	108
Michael Jordan	108
Michael Moore	76 (quote)
Michael Schumacher	70
Michelangelo	105-106, 105 (quote)
Mother Teresa	57 (quote)
Muhammad Ali	135 (quote)
new year resolutions	82-83
Nicholas Butler	131 (quote)
Nick Matthew	73-75, 145
Noah Weinberg	16 (quote)
'Now Discover Your Strengths' book	40
Oprah Winfrey	70, 112 (quote)
Orison Swett Marsden	28 (quote)
'Outliers' book	101
outsourcing	62-63
Pablo Picasso	20 (quote)
Paul Coelho	1 (quote)
Peggy Fleming	6 (quote)
Phil Taylor	70
Plato	69 (quote)
PSA	12-16
Queen Elizabeth II	6
Rafael Nadal	46, 52, 55, 95, 96, 97, 100
Ray Dalio	91, 100
Rene Lavand	39 (quote)
Richard Branson	4, 63, 82, 128 (quote)
Richard Desmond	70

risk/reward balance	59-60	Steve Peters	84 (quote)
Robert Collier	7 (quote)	Steven Pressfield	71 (quote)
Robert Greene	69 (quote), 80 (quote)	Stuart Wilde	133 (quote)
Robert Ingersoll	129 (quote)	success definition	1
Robert Vallerand	138	super-strength	2, 18, 48, 60, 61, 67-80, 112, 115, 126
Rodney Dangerfield	110		
Roger Federer	44, 46, 51 (quote), 52, 55, 70, 94-96, 108, 118	'Talent is Overrated' book	102
		The Beatles	104
		The Body Shop	78
Ryan Khan	62 (quote)	The Gap	110
Sam Walton	110-111	Thomas Fuller	86 (quote)
Samuel Johnson	37 (quote)	Tiger Woods	107
Scranton University	82	Titanic	6
Serena Williams	97, 100, 107-108	Tony Robbins	4, 101 (quote), 117 (quote), 146
setbacks	20, 61, 81, 88, 111, 117-120, 122, 125-128, 142		
		triggers (positive and negative)	35, 57
		U2	124
'So good they can't ignore you' book	112	Under Armour	76-78
Sophia Amoruso	30 (quote)	Usain Bolt	97, 100
Squash	5-17, 73-75, 145	USP	2, 31, 32, 44, 68, 71, 78, 79, 131
Stan Slap	129 (quote)		
Stanford University	92	Venus Williams	97, 107
Steve Jobs	12 (quote), 118 (quote)	Vera Wang	109
		Vince Lombardi	116 (quote)
Steve Maraboli	1 (quote), 50 (quote)	Vincent Van Gogh	36 (quote)

Wal-Mart 110-111

Warren Buffett 4, 134 (quote)

Wayne Dyer 15 (quote)

Wayne Gretzky 3 (quote)

Whatsapp 120-121

Whipp's Tiered Talents 44-47, 49, 79

Wimbledon Tennis Championships 52, 71-73, 75, 100

Winston Churchill 125 (quote), 127 (quote)

Zig Ziglar 19 (quote)

DISCLAIMER

The text within this eBook are the author's personal thoughts. The facts used are as a result of real research by a particular party. It could be possible that alternative research is available.

The contents of this eBook are not intended to be a definitive set of instructions. You may discover there are other methods and materials to accomplish the same end result.
Generally this advice helps people but it is not a guarantee of success or even wealth. There are no promises.

Printed in Great Britain
by Amazon